MEMOIRS OF
A MENDICANT PROFESSOR

MEMOIRS OF A MENDICANT PROFESSOR

D. J. Enright

1969
CHATTO & WINDUS
LONDON

Published by
Chatto & Windus Ltd
42 William IV Street
London W.C.2

★

Clarke, Irwin & Co. Ltd
Toronto

SBN 7011 1408 8
© D. J. Enright 1969
Printed in Great Britain by
Cox & Wyman Ltd,
London, Fakenham and Reading

For
MY STUDENTS

'I advise our descendants to be born with thick skins on their backs.'
Heine

'A small bird who was being strangled by a hawk had only time for one last loud protesting cry of indignation. But in that cry, brief as it was, it felt it had fulfilled its being, and its little soul made boast of it as it flew up towards the sun and was lost in the azure sky.'
Italo Svevo

'My philosophy is, there are more things in heaven and earth than are dreamt of in my philosophy.'
Tao Tschung Yu

Contents

CONTENTS

Foreword, Forearmed

Once again the Year of the Monkey is here.
I was born in the Year of the Monkey –
Surely a fellow can talk about himself a bit,
in his own year?

THESE memoirs do not 'cover' either time or place, but
in time they relate to the period between 1956 and 1967
and in place to Berlin, Bangkok and Singapore, except for
an initial scattering of flashbacks to Japan and the three years
between 1953 and 1956, and of course an occasional brief
sojourn between engagements in London, sometimes spring-
board and sometimes mattress.

When I look back over them, it strikes me that these
memoirs might perhaps be more aptly entitled Misfortunes
or Misadventures – though not, I hope, with much propriety,
Miseries. If this is so, the reason does not lie entirely in the
author's melancholy cast of mind or his proneness to the lesser
class of accident. For happiness and success are private matters,
whereas misfortune and failure appear to have more of the
public about them, they are of wider relevance, they partake
more of what we call 'our time'. Weep, and a large part of the
world will have reason to weep with you; laugh, and you
laugh alone. Happiness is timeless and universal, whereas mis-
haps are more distinctively of one specific time and place. And
whatever has happened to me, if it holds any interest at all, is
interesting because it *happened*, not because it happened to *me*.
My excuse for using the word 'I' so shamefully often must be
that a lot of the time it bears the sense of 'eye'.

I must say at once that I have no intention of weeping at
excessive length or with any pronounced degree of desolation.
Since we have spoken of misfortune and misery, it would be
fitting to recognize that the person who hasn't been beaten

to death or gassed or starved or imprisoned for long years, and hasn't had cause to mourn someone who has suffered this not so uncommon fate, should regard himself as fortunate. And the man who can sit down at the typewriter to compose his memoirs, reasonably sure of the next meal and the next month, should consider himself so unusually happy as to wonder whether he has anything of public interest to write about.

2

Against Authorship

I T was an evening in Summer 1956, and we had recently arrived in London from Japan. We had expected that we would be going next to Egypt, back to Egypt, to Alexandria, where my wife had been offered her old post at the Lycée Français and I was to take some sort of visiting professorship at the university. It was now called the University of Alexandria, but I had known it as Farouk I University when I taught there in a lowly capacity between 1947 and 1950. At some stage during the voyage from Japan, my wife had received a brief and cryptic note from the Directeur of the Lycée Français to the effect that, because of *le livre que vous savez*, I was no longer *persona grata* with the Egyptians. I couldn't quite understand the reference to the book which we knew of – it was true that early the previous year I had published a novel about Egypt, but it was not the sort of book to upset the Egyptians, I would have said, nor were the Egyptians the sort of people to be upset by a book. But we understood that we were in London, with no job, little in the way of savings, and nowhere to live outside the hotel into which we had moved on arrival. The greater part of our belongings lay in bond in Tilbury Docks.

On this particular evening we were sitting in a restaurant with a friend, a member of the British Diplomatic Service who had also returned from Japan recently. It was an oriental-style restaurant off Charing Cross Road, for we were indulging a nostalgia for the Far East made all the sharper by the feeling that no other part of the world was keen to harbour us. My wife and I had spent three years, teaching French literature and English literature respectively, at a comparatively small and relatively private university in the Kansai, that especially rewarding region which takes in Kobe, Osaka and Kyoto. We had not been sponsored or subsidized by any

13

outside agency, but Kōnan University was notably generous to us, considering the low level of the salaries paid to our Japanese colleagues. Japan can enchant or appal, but it never bores, it never leaves one indifferent. Those three years we had loved and hated, and obviously a change was needed, for one cannot alternate between the heights and the depths for long. Or so we had thought before we landed in London.

At the next table in the restaurant sat a group of Japanese businessmen, likewise indulging themselves in that nostalgia for Japan which the Japanese experience more acutely than anyone else. Our diplomatic friend went over to their table and addressed them in Japanese, which he spoke fluently, though his delivery always reminded me of the stylized intonations of the Kabuki theatre. He introduced himself and then mentioned my name. A small chorus of sounds of recognition arose, carefully washed of emotional tone, and the Japanese gentlemen got up and made rather hurriedly, I thought, for the door. One of them lagged behind, shook me surreptitiously by the hand and said, '*Enraito sensei*, I like the book you have written about Japan, but many do not.' And he too vanished into Irving Street.

It struck me then, as it was to strike me more forcibly on several later occasions, that it was rather saddening to get into trouble because of some book or article or poem which apparently no one had read except the people with whom one thereupon got into trouble.

Though in fact the Japanese were extremely polite and forbearing about my book on the Japanese. In 1955 there was still something of the post-war spirit of self-correction, or at least of correction, in the atmosphere, and my first and last mentor, Dr. Jugaku, had assured me that my criticisms would be acceptable to intellectuals, though not everyone (he regretted) was an intellectual. The only published review of *The World of Dew* I saw in Japan was patiently complimentary, while regretting that I had not lived longer in the country before judging it and that I was not a Buddhist, since I was thus unqualified to comprehend the Japanese attitude towards human life. I was myself conscious of the book's deficiencies, and I suspected that part of its acerbity was prompted less by Japanese attitudes and customs than by the sheer slop which was being published on the subject at the time. Slop, I hasten to say, from other foreign pens. As a British reviewer pointed out, the tone of the book was governessy; and I suppose, not being a cat or a dog, I should have refrained from complaining of Japanese callousness towards the sufferings of animals. This particular error at least was rectified by a later visiting writer, who adduced as dumb witnesses to the local love of animals those dogs who lie stretched confidently out on Japanese roads while the traffic swirls around them.

While I suspect they often feel an appropriate contempt for the foreign observer, the Japanese are (or were) extremely sensitive to the comments of foreign visitors in general and in particular of visiting poets, since the latter are held to be non-political and in other ways superior observers. This sensitiveness was by no means simply a question of desiring praise and approbation, for at times they appeared to welcome, in a masochistic way, the very opposite. Possibly this was to some extent a post-war attitude, for it was the era of the Kindly American in Asia, of Lafcadio Hearn *redivivus*, and Japanese intellectuals couldn't but feel aggrieved when they saw the small cultured Nipponese being patted on his head for those age-old virtues which they themselves considered the agents of social and mental oppression and the auxiliaries of militarism.

We were between wars, and another enemy had loomed up. Bigger, as enemies always seem to be. Before long we were to see much the same situation in Berlin, as between the Germans and the British, but on a smaller scale and in a limited and military context, for the British cannot quite achieve the American self-debasement in the face of an alien culture, nor did the Germans care half as much as the Japanese what their former enemies and conquerors now thought of them. The division of Germany, the division of Berlin and the isolation of West Berlin were presumably more potent, more conclusive arguments, too, than Hiroshima and Nagasaki. The atomic bombs had only gone off once.

Soon after my book on Japan I published a collection of poems almost entirely concerned with that country, and I piously hoped that the poems, with their greater sympathy for the ordinary Japanese, would be read in conjunction with the prose account and so serve to offset the latter's priggishness and its deficiencies of imagination. It is a common delusion in writers to suppose that readers will see their publications as they see them. In this instance I was being exceptionally naïve, for the poems were read only by people who read poems, not by people who read travel books, and the poems were read as poems – as artefacts, as things-in-themselves and not as writings-about-Japan. Not surprisingly, as artefacts, as aesthetic constructions, they proved unsatisfactory. Subject-matter dropped out of poetry some time back; the art has drawn in upon itself increasingly, self-nurtured and consequently sickly, sick with the sickness of our time, when the best lack all convictions excepting those readily expressible in words of four letters.

When you have written a book about a country, for you the book becomes the country. You cannot really bring yourself to believe that the country may not be quite like that, or that it has changed since, or will ever change. You have written about it, you have embalmed it. At the best it will be difficult for you to look at the country again, because the book keeps getting in the way. Here, in the next few pages, I have attempted to look round the book by summoning up incidents and persons disconnected and diverse enough, I hope, to discourage any thesis from emerging or re-emerging. I start with an account of two trips to Hiroshima which were made after I had drafted my book on Japan, and which in any case could not have been included there without an effect of peculiar heartlessness.

3

Hiroshima — Make Coffee not War

Is the dust, sweeping down like an ambush,
To be seen today, too?
Does it fall today, too?
Is the great cage, swinging about like dust,
To be seen today, too?

EISAKU YONEDA

THE first trip must have been in 1954. The English Department of Hiroshima University, finding they had a little
money in the kitty, invited me to give a few lectures. To begin
with I was accommodated in a very pleasant Japanese-style
inn. On my first evening we had dinner there, Professor
Michio Masui, a Chaucerian of considerable repute, some of
his colleagues and myself. After dinner the maid cleared the
table and pulled out the *futon*, the mattress, on which I was
to spend the night. My fellow academics had left, but it was
not yet nine o'clock. The maid mistook my incredulous expression for one of incomprehension, and she pointed politely
but firmly to the mattress. Since there was no option, I crawled
under the covers and passed the night in a state of quivering
insomnia.

I asked my friends the next day whether it was compulsory
or customary to retire so early in Hiroshima. They held a
whispered conference, and the remaining evenings we spent
in a swift and confusing succession of bars and night-clubs.
On each occasion the most junior member of the party paid
the bill and kept an account of what was spent; my efforts to
contribute something were always courteously but resolutely
repulsed. Clearly some of the company had never entered
such places before, but equally clearly they enjoyed this new
experience. I was for ever touched by the mutual respect and
concern which flowed between bar girls and teachers in Japan.

The girls would take care to see that no one got drunk and that the bill should be as small as possible, for they knew that the customers' earnings were likely to be even smaller than their own. If there was something rather conscious and strained in the professors' scrupulous politeness and posture of extreme but utterly platonic interest – I have a photograph taken in one of these Hiroshima bars which looks like a daguerreotype of the staff and senior pupils of an earnest Victorian school for girls – at least there was none of that business of 'how did you come to take up this work?' But then, the answer was obvious, simple and true: poverty. There was no sin, not in Hiroshima, but only necessity.

In one bar, I remember, I was dancing with a handsome and unusually well-built girl, who asked me, '*Kohi shimas'ka?*' – Shall we make coffee? Her intention was so patently good-hearted that I was quite moved, and went to some trouble to explain that, much as I liked the stuff during the day, I found that I couldn't sleep after it in the evening. I didn't want a repetition of that first night in the Atomic City. 'So?' she responded sympathetically, and we continued to dance. Fondly recalling the girl's considerateness the next morning, it suddenly struck me that it was not *kohi* she had proposed to make, but *koi*, a word rather similar in pronunciation but having the meaning of 'love between man and woman'.

In Hiroshima at that time, I should imagine, any visitor not of the most zealously touristic or scientifically curious disposition would be likely to be afflicted with insomnia. The new makeshift houses were already drab and decrepit, the Atomic Bomb Souvenir Shop was a modern ruin, the Peace Park was largely mud during my visit, and the various other commemorative objects sited about the centre of the explosion appeared rather to have fallen under the bomb than to have been raised in its memory. No doubt by now this whole area has been trimmed into the properly and safely historical, but at that date it was all too contemporaneous, as if the survivors had only had time and strength to shift some of the debris around to make an impromptu cairn. No doubt the present Atomic Bomb Museum is a museum in the accepted sense of the word, a clean and sober structure housing a smart and orderly collection of exhibits in glass cases, labelled accurately and grammatically in a number of languages, and furnished with benches for visitors whose feet are beginning to pain them. No doubt it is more instructive than the original little museum, and a good deal less horrifying, and much less admonitory. Pointing backwards, not forwards.

The museum as I saw it was a smallish building of mean and makeshift appearance, and its interior was at first reminiscent of those haphazard and dusty aquariums so commonly to be found in small towns in Japan, perhaps marking the strong maritime strand in the national character, perhaps in deference to the passionate Japanese appetite for information of any kind. An aquarium? No, rather a junk shop. Tiles melted out of shape and a few fried shoes dumped on a trestle table. Some second-hand tombstones in poor condition, several oddly grained blocks of granite, a bicycle which had apparently been left out in the sun too long and had melted and reset in a different shape. Some humorous photographs, not too well defined, of atomic tricks, of the shadow of a spiral staircase imprinted by the atomic flash on the side of a gas tank and of the upper slab of a tomb which had been lifted by the blast and fell back to trap a flying stone; some less amusing photographs of the shadows left behind by pedestrians crossing a bridge and by somebody sitting on the steps of a bank when the bomb exploded, and a photograph of the pattern of a dress left on the wearer's back; also some unfunny but happily indistinct photographs of scorched and corrugated flesh. And hanging on the wall, a shabby pair of the baggy trousers worn by women workers, with an explanation scrawled underneath: 'The lady who weared this *mompei* was working 1,300 meters away from the center of the explosion.' The seat of the trousers was badly burnt.

On the way out, passing over the little badges decorated with a stodgy dove and the letters 'H.P.S.' for Hiroshima Peace Society, I purchased a souvenir brochure packed with statistics and mathematical calculations, which among other things described with no trace of irony how the location of the epicentre and hypocentre of the explosion was determined by examining the exfoliation or surface mutation on tombstones situated in different sections of the city and then backtracking the heat rays. As I left, I realized that the tank filled with ashes at the door was not a refuse bin but a model of Hiroshima as it looked directly after the bomb had fallen.

The Atomic Cenotaph resembles in shape a hump-backed bridge. I was told that it represented a saddle, or rather one of those clay images which were set around the tombs of the ancient emperors when the custom of burying live servants, real saddles and so forth had come to seem too painful or too expensive. The aptness of this choice of a shape perhaps lies in the fact that the saddle exactly frames the near-by ruins which mark the hypocentre of the explosion. Within the saddle is an altar, and on the altar an inscription which none of my friends and informants was able to explicate very precisely. 'Please sleep peacefully, for we do not repeat our faults' – or so it might be translated. But the noun *ayamachi* possesses a range of meanings, from 'blunder' down to 'crime'. Nor is it clear what the fault or mistake was or who committed it. No doubt the author of the inscription meant something and meant well, but its ambiguity is certainly convenient. Everyone who passes by, patriot, penitent or pacifist, victor or vanquished, American tourist or Japanese sightseer, Leftist or Rightist, everyone can interpret it to his own satisfaction.*

There are other Atomic monuments in the Peace Park, among them two naïvely modernistic Bridges of Peace, a

* Not quite everyone, according to Robert Jungk, who reports in *Children of the Ashes* that some of the bereaved objected to the possible implication that it was the dead who had committed faults or mistakes.

fragile-looking Children's Library and the glass-and-chrom-
ium Hotel New Hiroshima, the latter catering for tourists and
participants in conferences. I was to have spent my last night
in this hotel – this was part of my hosts' careful planning – and
I was rather looking forward to it as a change from the slightly
forbidding régime of the inn, which in some ways was a
museum, though a scrupulously clean one, of the domestic
traditions of Japan. It was not to be. One of our academic party
was a young New Zealander, teaching in a girls' college,
whose mother had just arrived to spend a little time with him.
The young man's declared ambition was to become the new
Lafcadio Hearn, a curious aspiration to pursue in these sur-
roundings one would have thought, and he had certainly
learnt a lot about Japanese ways (rather too much, I suspect,
for the liking of the Japanese, who prefer foreigners to be
foreign and in need of instruction, enlightenment and guid-
ance) and was already proficient in the more idiomatic aspects
of the language. His alarmed mother had come to seek to
persuade him to return to his native heath, and whether it
was maternal distress caused by his tatamization or by the
sights of Hiroshima and its ubiquitous dust I do not know,
but the lady suffered a mild heart attack directly outside
the hotel. So I gave her my room in the hotel and spent
the night on the *tatami* floor of the young man's small
wooden house.

At that time there were still other commemorative objects
in evidence. The day after I reached Hiroshima a boy of nine-
teen died of radiation disease, and the day I left saw the departure for America of twenty-five girls suffering from keloid
disfigurement which it was hoped to alleviate by plastic surgery. The project, sponsored by the (American) Committee
to Aid the Girls of Hiroshima, had given rise to a good deal
of varied ill-feeling. The Hiroshima local paper considered
that the Americans should treat every casualty since it was
their bomb which had caused all the damage, but it had to be
satisfied with exhorting the selected girls to adopt a firm
attitude and stand for no action, even in jest, 'which would

tend to make them an object of curiosity'. From an American newspaper man came the complaint that the project was just another illustration of the truth that one way of winning a war was to lose it to the U.S.A. – a proposition which in this setting grows more ludicrous (to say the least) the more one studies it. Later I came across a news item concerning the arrival of the 'Maidens of Hiroshima' in San Francisco which related how four women calling themselves representatives of 'The Northern California Peace Council' turned up at the airport and indicated their wish to make a speech on outlawing the H-bomb. 'They were not permitted to take part in the welcoming ceremonies.'

Strolling through the town I came across yet another commemorative object. Rather than distress memory I prefer to quote a description jotted down at the time. 'A man, I suppose, propped up on the pavement in the shape of a St. Andrew's cross, on one leg and the remnant of an arm to which a strip of wood had been fixed. The head, and the stump of the other arm, hung at an angle of a hundred degrees to the ground. The face had been deeply tanned by the "atomic sun". He appeared to be asleep (rather, he appeared to be long dead), and from the closed mouth hung a few motionless green leaves.'

On our way to the station and the train that would take me back to the milder Kansai, the professor intimated in gently embarrassed style that he feared there was nothing left of the fee they had intended to offer me for the lectures. It had all gone on our nocturnal outings. We were all gratified, they because they knew I would best enjoy this mode of remuneration, I because they were right about that and because I was relieved to know they hadn't ruined themselves in riotous living at my instigation. Shall we make coffee? Or – come to that – love? We might as well, even if it leads to insomnia, for it was difficult to sleep peacefully in Hiroshima.

·   ·   ·   ·   ·

My second visit to Hiroshima must have taken place a few months before the tenth anniversary of the bomb on August 6, 1955. A group of writers and well-wishers in the city planned to bring out a booklet of 'bomb poems' in the original with English translations, and I had been co-opted to help with the translations. This only involved me in ironing out a few unnecessary obscurities and inapt linguistic eccentricities in the final drafts, and I was particularly glad to do what I could since most of the poems (all of them by people who had been in Hiroshima at the time) were written by 'ordinary citizens' who normally would not have written poetry or certainly would not have written poetry of so distinctly 'modern' a kind. The traditional Japanese style, the customary calm and remote meditativeness, could not cope with this extraordinary experience. There was some similarity in this respect with the poetry written by Wilfred Owen and others, or written by the war, during the First World War. Unlike so much Japanese verse, these poems came out of a particular event, a shared event, and not a time-hallowed and acceptedly literary state of mind.

Songs of Hiroshima appeared in time, indeed before more than two of its contributors were dead. Copies of the booklet were sent to British periodicals, but as far as I am aware no one took any notice of it. In the mid-1950's the British poetry-reading public, or at any rate the editorial side of it, didn't want any more poems about Hiroshima. In a note written (amusingly enough) for an anthology published in Tokyo in that same year, Kingsley Amis remarked that nobody (he hoped) wanted any more poems about philosophers or paintings or mythology or foreign cities. His meaning seemed perfectly plain to me. Such were the subjects most favoured by bad or non-poets; and the imaginary titles Mr. Amis listed in his poem 'Something Nasty in the Bookshop' were the sort of titles which commonly heralded one species of pretentious nonsense one didn't want any more of. 'Landscape near Parma', 'The Double Vortex', 'Rilke and Buddha' . . . Rather a good poem about changing the baby's nappy – or so I take it Mr. Amis intended – than a bad poem about Rilke or God or Venice or Hiroshima. Unfortunately this admonition chimed with and served to confirm that British parochialism, the mock-modesty of the Little Englanders, which had been on the increase since the end of the war. In poetry its principle seemed to be, rather a bad poem about changing the baby's nappy than a good poem about Parma or Buddha or Hiroshima. Yet if the 'Movement' poets in retrospect look stodgy and prissily over-prudent, then as regards subject-matter they were almost Homeric in comparison with more recent writers. While Japanese poets have been struggling to escape from the greenhouse of the haiku's brief and stereotyped profundities into the Western poet's larger and more public world, Anglo-American poets have been retreating into the tenuous and tremulous delicatenesses of the haiku. And without quite getting there.

Again funds were low in Hiroshima. This was a long time ago. Now of course one would be able to pick and choose among Foundations and Agencies all eager to meet one's expenses, and even the C.I.A. might be willing to sponsor such a project, if only to save the old bomb from becoming a Communist property. So Miyao Ohara, the editor of the booklet and a teacher at a local girls' college, arranged for me to stay with Dr. K—, who was working in Hiroshima when the bomb fell and had written a book about his experiences. Dr. K— was a breezy, open and assured personality, much more like a successful businessman than like the inhibited, anguished and wholly introverted members of the teaching profession with whom I had most to do. He was certainly a busy man and I saw little of him except at breakfast, which was a mammoth and international exercise, embracing the British variety, the continental variety and the local version. I don't think this medley was arranged for my benefit. I eat very little breakfast at the best of times. But Dr. K— ranged from dish to dish and culture to culture with gusto and impartiality.

'Come,' he had addressed me briskly as I lay in my room,

'Put on a *yukata* and let us go down to breakfast. The women will bring your clothes down while we are eating.' The women were his wife and a maid of about fifteen years. They knelt on the sideline and encouraged us in our dealings with the breakfast, and then they proceeded to dress us. Dr. K— stood there among the dishes, naked and unashamed and royally bellied, while the two women dressed him with the absorbed expressions of window-dressers draping a mannequin. I tried to recover my clothing and rush up to my room, but in vain: I was temporarily one of the family and thus subject to the proper male prerogatives. Having finished with the master, the ladies turned to me and, with a discernible increase in interest, whipped my *yukata* over my shrinking shoulders. It is well known that nudity is a matter of absolutely no concern in Japan. That sounds splendid. But this traditional attitude does not extend to foreigners: with them nudity is known to be a matter of concern, whether the nudity is someone else's or their own. Moreover, the Japanese are not yet altogether satisfied that Westerners are constructed after quite the same design as they are; indeed, since the Japanese are unique, it is hardly to be expected that foreigners will be structurally identical. I remember many a time, sitting by glum and unwanted, while bar-girls were fussing intimately over my wife. 'Fancy that, two breasts . . . just like us!'

And so, with the wariness of a true 'Movement' poet, I had stealthily slipped on my under-pants before going down to breakfast, while Dr. K— wasn't watching. The sounds of proleptic admiration from the two women were abruptly cut off. I felt ashamed of myself when I saw the calamitous drooping of the servant-girl's mouth. It was an unkind trick to play. '*So des*!' murmured the wife, remembering her manners and making the best of it, 'How white your skin is!' as she nipped my arm between her fingers and rubbed the skin like someone appraising a length of dubious silk.

The publication committee had also arranged for me to

attend a Rotary Club luncheon in the Hotel New Hiroshima,
not because of any connection existing between myself and
Rotary or between Rotary and the Hiroshima poets. It was
a free lunch, and money, as I have mentioned, was in short
supply. But before lunch I was to meet one of the contributors
to the *Songs*, a young lady. The two best-known of our fifteen
poets were dead; Sankichi Toge had died two years before,
of an old lung malady aggravated by radiation damage, and
Tamiki Hara killed himself in 1951, fearing that the Korean
war would develop into total nuclear conflict. There was a
second woman contributor, but she was a poverty-stricken
widow, and thus (I suppose) less presentable to a visiting
aesthete. Miss Setsuko Harada, besides being available, was a
direct victim of the bomb. She was a nurse, who had been in
hospital under treatment for the past five years, and my
associates proposed to collect her from the hospital and bring
her to the lobby of the hotel in order that I should meet her
and be thanked for helping with the English version of her
poem. I protested strenuously against this barbarous courtesy.
I was quite ready to go unthanked, especially as I had done
so very little. I was also quite ready to go without seeing
any more dreadful sights, particularly if I were to con-
sume a Rotary Club lunch immediately thereafter. But,
as ever in these contests of politeness with the Japanese, I
lost.

The press-gang arrived with Miss Harada in a taxi exactly
as the lunch was commencing, and I had only time to take her
hand and she had insufficient time to say her thank-you
properly. She would, I was told, wait until lunch was over.
I agitated for the privilege of taking her in and sharing my
lunch with her: but no, I was told, ladies were not allowed
into meetings of the Rotary Club. I agitated for the privilege
of taking her out to lunch: but no, I was told, I couldn't lunch
out because I was lunching with the Rotary Club, it had been
arranged. Miss Harada could wait, she might as well wait in
the lobby of the hotel as in the hospital, she had nothing to do
but wait.

I wasn't to escape completely without working my passage. There was the usual array of banners and pennants in the dining-room, and the usual stream of greetings from here and there. To my alarm I was called upon to add to this stream, and in my extremity I recalled my sole previous encounter with Rotary, when in my capacity as an extra-mural organizing tutor for the Black Country I had spoken briefly on D. H. Lawrence to a lunch meeting of the Cradley Heath branch – or was it Brierley Hill? Or Old Hill? (I remember that afterwards one of the lunchers had indicated dissatisfaction: 'I always heard this chap wrote sort of *hot* stuff!') So I informed the gathering that I brought them the fraternal greetings of the chain-makers and nail-makers of Cradley Heath, Staffordshire, England.

When I made my escape from lunch it was time for Miss Harada to report back to the hospital. She bowed and I smiled, which wasn't difficult, for the only visible signs of the bomb were slightly raised chalk-white scar tissues on her arms. Miss Harada was in her early twenties, her face was of that extreme pallor to be found among Japanese and Chinese but never, apart from an occasional death-bed, in the lands of the White races. She was a humble, uneducated person, certainly not (like Toge and Hara) a professional writer; she was one of those who had been compelled into poetry by their experiences at the time or directly afterwards. Her poem in the book was called 'Square Rain is Tapping':

> *Square rain is tapping*
> *On your motor-hearse of white;*
> *White rain*
> *Mingled with the twentieth century's dust,*
> *Tapping on your car of white.*
>
> *You who've come back to the coffin*
> *Show us once again*
> *The anger of Hiroshima.*
> *Your voice from the crevice of the coffin,*
> *Give off to us your scent.*

Creaking away from the raining gate
The motor-hearse leaves its sound
Echoing about the hospital,
About Hiroshima, spreading about Hiroshima's sky!

4

Japanese Miscellany

MEMORIES after eleven years? Sufficient of them, and sufficiently vivid, to make a return trip seem incongruous (the mountains might have been flattened, the abysses filled in) and a holiday as a tourist utterly out of the question.

Above all memories of innumerable acts of kindness, of desires met before they were expressed (and even, sometimes, felt), of debts of hospitality painfully irredeemable, of a patience almost infuriating, of a pervasive effort to fit in with foreign prejudices, to create for the stranger a sense of that humanism or humanitarianism which among themselves they could barely afford. In Japan even starving animals make an attempt to look cheerful and fit when a foreigner comes into sight. Almost.

But I must emphasize that I am not writing a travel book – these are memoirs, and at this point they go back eleven years. Since then Japan has prospered, and perhaps its people have too.

For my memories are of people rather than of places, though Japan is famous for its places rather than its people. And first among them, the judicious Dr. Bunshō Jugaku, my original and prime mentor, who knew when to let go of the guiding strings; a specialist in English literature, deeply and widely read, whose dream of England was superior to the reality, or at all events to the reality which he would have found there. Happily he was past the age for travelling scholarships!

S-san, another teacher, middle-aged and untiring, whose brother worked for a company doing business with France, so that regularly S-san would turn up at our house, impressively early in the morning, with yet another letter for my wife to translate. 'A French letter!' he would cry in his loud healthy voice outside our bedroom, 'I have brought the madam another French letter!' I couldn't bring myself to explain the idiomatic usage of this phrase to him, even though it was my proper duty to do so; nor did any of our mutual colleagues to whom I related this unhappy misunderstanding feel able to act as go-between. It would have meant such a grievous loss of face for S-san. Eventually we found ourselves, minds cleansed of the idiomatic, speaking quite naturally of S-san's brother's French letters.

Haruko, a beautiful and civilized girl, who was employed as a maid in an English household in Tokyo, and became a pet, a companion and finally a full member of the family. Some years earlier Haruko had cut off her hair and posted it to a returned Australian soldier who had given her the impression that he had matrimony in mind. The cutting-off of the hair signified that she considered herself a widow and had no intention of re-marrying. Later, under the benign influence of her English family, she changed her mind, like a sensible girl, and married – married another foreigner, I think. (My wife tells me that this was not so, and that Haruko left Japan in the company of a foreign Lesbian. I prefer my ending.)

Those anonymous students and their rented tape-recorders (often paid for by the sale of blood to transfusion centres) who would arrive at one's house early on a Sunday morning, or simultaneously with S-san and his foreign correspondence, so that one might be good enough to record in one's pure and undefiled English another thirty pages of some primer consisting of silly questions and even sillier answers, or perhaps the second half of *Black Beauty* or the first half of the *Private Papers of Henry Ryecroft*. Polite but determined, they would hear nothing of illness or exhaustion, for such were taken as read, such were the accustomed lot of both learners and teachers. Disinclination was not considered to exist, except as a curious foreign joke, to be smiled at and disregarded.

Much less grim, the girls at Tsuda College, a university for women subsidized by an American mission board, several miles outside Tokyo. When a male went there to lecture – or did it have to be a foreign male? – the students would lurk in the corridors, hoping to catch him alone, just for the sake of a few innocent words in conversation. 'A man!' they would sigh noisily, 'We want to talk to a man! We are tired of these dried-up old lady-teachers!' Highly gratifying, of course. These lively girls were going to be journalists or novelists, or they were going into broadcasting or television, they were going to revolutionize Japanese society. None of them was intending to become a teacher. But more vividly I remember their teachers, those dried-up old maids, American-trained or Cambridge Ph.D.s, the *samurai* of female education, who had gone much further in revolutionizing society than any of these lively young ladies were likely to go.

And an old maid of another sort. Our faithful domestic, Okamoto-san, who we realized was a Christian only when we became aware of the prayer-meetings which she held in her small *tatami*-floored room (all the better to pray on) along with our five-year-old daughter. These meetings, we found, were occasionally devoted to the theme of the Atomic Bomb. Okamoto-san had discovered the book I brought back from Hiroshima, with its photographs of the ruins, human and otherwise, and she was using this as a textbook. What the text was I cannot imagine. The wrath of God as illustrated in this foretaste opportunely administered by a Christian nation to a non-Christian one? I doubt it. When, rather nervously, we questioned our daughter, she merely explained in a solemn voice that the pictures were of people burnt by the Americans. Okamoto-san was extremely attached to her, and never failed to come between the dragon and his wrath, at moments of dissension snatching the child to her small bosom and out-facing the master of the house. The child returned these feelings, and for some time she believed that the well-known carol was composed in honour of her friend, mentor and protector. 'Okamoto faithful, joyful and triumphant . . .'

The formidable T-san, the most liberal of hosts during our first months in Japan, who owned a castle, furnished half in

Japanese style and half in Western style, and accommodated us in the latter half until the university bought a house for us. The first modern tycoon in a family series of Osaka merchants whose portraits ranged in style from wood-block prints up to Royal Academy oils, he had given his employees a union after the war, when unions became fashionable, even though he himself couldn't see the practical use of it. A tough businessman who didn't for a moment dream of pretending that he wasn't the boss (any more than he would pretend not to be drunk when he was: on those rare occasions it was the sober bystander who lost face), he was also an enthusiastic and knowledgeable orchid-grower.

The man in a bar who refused to recognize the cessation of hostilities and informed me that I was his enemy and in his opinion he was still fighting me. Whereupon he fell off his stool, was tenderly taken up by solicitous bar-girls, brushed down, had the last and smallest fallen coin restored to his pockets, and (his address having been ascertained from papers in his wallet) was borne into a taxi, his patriotic exclamations drowned beneath the consoling hum of the girls, who knew that the war was over, or hoped it was.

Another, rather better-class, bar in Tokyo, in which, late at night and late in a hard night's work, a complicated problem of 'face' arose. As often happened, the girls had remarked on my likeness to Danny Kaye – he was very popular in Japan at this time, largely because of his work for UNICEF if I remember correctly – and Bill McAlpine, a friend of mine working for the British Council, insisted that in fact I was Danny Kaye. The girls believed him, or pretended to believe him because it would have been impolite to doubt his word. I, since my friend had stated that I was Danny Kaye, could not politely repudiate this ascription of identity, and being an admirer of the actor, I felt little inclination to do so. Much later, as we were about to leave, several of the girls came up with their spare handkerchiefs for Danny Kaye to sign. If I were to sign in this capacity then I would be telling a lie, and also spoiling their handkerchiefs for nothing. On the other hand, if I didn't sign, then I was proclaiming my friend a liar, and what was worse, a successful liar, in that the girls had believed him or at least had acted as if they believed him. Thus, and this was a graver consideration, I would also be exposing the girls to the considerable humiliation of being seen to have been deceived. Clearly, or fairly clearly – all these factors dizzied through my head as I reached slowly for my pen – the better course was to sign as requested and take the whole of this curious burden of minor guilt upon myself. There was a bad moment when I couldn't remember whether or not there was an 'e' at the end of my surname, but I think I got it right. At all events the girls were very pleased with their autographed handkerchiefs, and Bill was pleased with the unexpected longevity of his little joke. The bill, which arrived shortly afterwards, was (I recall) worthier of a Hollywood star than of a teacher.

The McAlpines, Bill and Helen, had arrived in Tokyo in November 1953, after a long sea voyage in a small cargo boat. I happened to be in Tokyo then, on my first visit to the capital, and had been invited out for the evening by some members of the Japan P.E.N. Club, hearty writers of *samurai* stories, some of them, and some of them swashbuckling drinkers, remote from one's conception of the Japanese aesthete. The McAlpines came along with us, and before long the fact that they hadn't recovered their land legs didn't make any difference. The details of the evening escape me, I can only remember vaguely a sequence of bars, hotel lounges, taverns, German-style beer-cellars (real steins and Japanese Fräuleins), drinking clubs and cabarets. I was staying at the same hotel as the McAlpines, so we had a last drink there and staggered to bed. I at once fell into a profound unconsciousness, from which I was reluctantly dragged some hours later by a violent sense of agitation. This was accompanied by unpleasant aural effects. I remembered then the warnings I had received against mixing saké with beer, not to mention

c

whisky. This was a peculiarly disturbing hangover – especially the way the bed seemed to be whipping about – and unusually fast in setting in. Then, for the walls of the hotel were thin, I heard urgent murmurings around me, the sounds of belts being hastily fastened and skirts dragged on, and then footsteps along the corridors. Standard practice in an earthquake of any dimension, as I knew, was to make for the porch, so that one could dodge out of the building or back into it as events prompted. So this was an earthquake, only an earthquake. The bed heaved again half-heartedly, and I relapsed contentedly into unconsciousness. Thank God, I could still hold my drink ... There was great excitement downstairs in the morning. 'The floor of the bathroom was actually corrugated, the tiles were like little waves ...' 'Have you noticed how freely the waste pipes run now?' 'And the toilet ... Nothing like a 'quake for unclogging the system!' Then the McAlpines came down, rosy-cheeked and ready for breakfast, eager to explore this new land. They hadn't noticed any earthquake; they had just sailed through several typhoons. That was my first earthquake. My second and slighter and last was in Kyoto, when we were dining with Donald Keene, the American Japanologist. He lived in the suburbs, in a more than commonly traditional Japanese house, and the room we were squatting in had an open fire for cooking with a chimney hood above it and lots of iron utensils hanging from the hood. These latter began to rattle, at first gently but with increasing force, apparently in time with a passing express train. I remarked that I hadn't known there was a railway line just outside. 'There isn't,' our host answered. Then the landlady came in to announce with quiet pride the presence of yet another Japanese tradition, the moving of the earth.

The constant attempt, too, to escape from tradition. Ninomiya-san, coming to my house once a week for another afternoon's unnerving tussle with modern Japanese poetry and its conveyance into English. Striving to decide what the original meant, how many meanings it might have, and which

of them if any – at least we could be sure that the poets themselves wouldn't be so uncouth as to breathe a word of complaint – we were going to struggle to reproduce or to produce
an inkling of in English. This was well before the great flood
of translations and imitations and projects and series, and
tenuous though their connection with the originals may be,
our versions at any rate held pioneer status. A selection of
them under the title *The Poetry of Living Japan* was published
in 1957 in the 'Wisdom of the East Series', a combination of
descriptions which at that time I'm afraid was considered a
contradiction in terms.

The Governor of the Prefecture, who gave a lunch in
honour of Edmund Blunden, then paying a short visit from
Hong Kong, at a celebrated teahouse which had earlier been
the summer residence of General Tojo. The eats were impeccable, the drinks eccentric, consisting of saké and beer and a
mysterious glass standing already full to the brim at each place,
which turned out to contain a mixture called Manhattan.
Casting back to his literary past in honour of the guest of
honour, the Governor divulged that before the war he had
been something of a playwright, he had produced a dramatization of the first chapter of *Das Kapital*. It seemed likely enough,
at this stage in the meal, anything seemed likely. The Blunden
daughters, healthy young English creatures, undisciplined
small foreign devils, scampered hither and thither, dashing
through the paper screens drawn round our room, leaving
artistic silhouettes of the Blunden daughters on General Tojo's
shoji, shadow puppets in reverse, a dramatization of the first
chapter of life. In fact, the Governor told us, his dramatization
of the first chapter of *Das Kapital* had been made into a film,
but the then government of Japan had banned it. 'The
militarists,' he sighed, 'Unhappy Japan! Unhappy times!'
We all felt satisfyingly sad about the past. Abruptly the
Governor rose and was gone, with the meal not yet at its end.
'A very busy man. He has been called to the office,' explained
two underlings from the Prefectural office, who had neither
eaten nor drunk. 'But I must thank him for his kindness,' I

said, making for the door. The underlings barred my way:
'A very busy man,' they smiled regretfully. 'I only wish to
thank him . . .' 'Thank you, thank you,' they said. As they
bowed their heads gratefully I glimpsed the Governor, out
in the courtyard, with two small geisha, one tucked under
each arm, dragging him swiftly towards his car, his feet
following reluctantly.

Akichan, who had a child, an old mother and a bedridden
consumptive husband to support, and no qualifications beyond those which fitted her to work in a dingy bar in the
labyrinth of Sannomiya, near the railway station in Kobe.
(Yes, I know, nothing but bar-girls and teachers, universities
and bars! But then, in Japan as elsewhere, the great middle
class was not to be known, kept itself to itself, would not
yield up its secrets. In any case, teachers and bar-girls make
up, or used to, quite a large section of the populace, and a
pretty likeable one.) Akichan was the steady girl-friend of a
young British diplomat, in this deceiving neither her mother
nor her dying husband. She used to talk sometimes of how
one day her third secretary would marry her, how one day
she would be the wife of an ambassador in Tokyo. It was hard
to tell if she believed this, or thought it a vague possibility,
or whether she said it to spare one's feelings, or herself. Her
good looks were fading, she would do nothing about the
decay in her front teeth (though I once offered to pay the
dentist's bill); and one day she had gone, without trace. And
her homely friend Sumichan, another kind-hearted girl, she
would never accept a tip which she considered the giver
couldn't afford, quite uncalculating, with nothing to look
forward to, often sad, yet never making you feel that it was
somehow your fault. Sumichan had a 'weak chest'. One day
she disappeared too, vaguely to 'the country' for her health,
leaving no address, for what use would that be? These girls
seemed to me instances of the most arrant, most heart-break-
ing wastage of human goodness which I had encountered
outside books. They still do. I wrote a poem about Akichan,
which in due course drew the scorn of a sharp English re-

viewer: I could, he pointed out as a measure of my sentimental falsification, 'even resurrect the myth of the good-hearted harlot'. Myth? He should just have said that it was a bad poem.

Another figure, which I met on a cold dark night in 1955, swathed from head to ankles in straw, the hands too, with a hood of sacking over the head and face –

What did I fear the most?
To ignore and bustle past?
To acknowledge and perhaps
Find out what best was lost?

– and have tried to exorcise by means of poems written at intervals ever since, but without success.

The Kabuki theatre, not so much a place as a congregation of people, and its pleasing, reassuring atmosphere, culture really being enjoyed for once. Old and young, with lunch-boxes open on their laps, shovelling the food down between cries of expert approbation, joy, distress or amusement. How grim the Western theatre is by comparison, with the audience strapped into their seats, programmes like watch-dogs on their laps, and the stage a mile away! A similar contrast is that between Thai temples, where you can squat down on the floor, tapping your cigarette ash into a chipped saucer, and wait for Buddha to find you in his own good time, and the churches of the Christians, in which one is bossed about by an adenoidally petulant official dressed in a garb half-way between a surgeon's outfit and baby-clothes.

The puppet theatre too, though by now it was something of a cult-object, more highbrow than Kabuki (whose actors are supposed to base their movements on those of the puppets), and especially Yamashiro-no-Shōjō, the celebrated chanter of the famous Osaka puppet theatre, who had recently been elevated alongside the palaces, temples, pagodas, pavilions, bells, images and imperial autographs known as Important Cultural Properties or National Treasures, under the slightly different designation of Human National Treasure. I have often been asked, accusingly, why my Japanese poems were so philistine, so vandalistic. Why did I get so worked up about the golden tonsils of Mr. Yamashiro-no-Shōjō? What did I have against him? I had nothing against him. I admired him as a great performer. I was glad that at last a human being was held to be a National Treasure, and I hoped that this was the beginning of a new era in which we would hear slightly less about temples and scrolls and a little more about people.

> *Let Mr. Yamashiro-no-Shōjō be heard in the lanes of Tophet,*
> *Let Mr. Yamashiro-no-Shōjō be honoured as a prophet,*

by all means. The blank unbridgeable chasm between an exquisite sensitivity towards the arts and a stolid insensitivity towards human suffering was just a little more than a Western softie like myself could accommodate. But in England things were very different of course, it was not people who suffered there, it was the arts and the intellect. And so my mutterings seemed strangely incongruous, an outburst of Kulturbolschevismus which left Apeneck Amis looking like a museum curator. When I pleaded my case with Donald Davie (who had reviewed my Japanese poems) he remarked that it was queer and not right that disagreement about a body of poems should resolve itself into conflicting diagnoses about what was wrong with English or with Japanese society, since that was the kind of thing which should concern us as intellectuals but not as poets. Yes, it was queer. I should have written the poems in Japanese, or else written them about England. Or better still, written aboutlessly.

Unforgettable was the microcosm of the Hankyū, the electric railway serving the largely middle-class stretch of country between Kobe and Osaka. The student who seizes the opportunity of eliciting a free English lesson from the horse's mouth. The American missionary of the 'Are you Saved?' variety, who can't speak even that much Japanese and seeks to justify his existence by swooping down on foreign passengers when for once they are not giving free language lessons to native students. The evening drunk, who turns red, then yellow, then dark green, then begins to groan, and the neatly-dressed lady who trots all the way from the far end of the carriage, spreads a newspaper between the sufferer's feet, bows modestly and retires. The bare-breasted peasant woman with a baby, whom everyone painstakingly ignores, except the embarrassed conductor who (with eyes averted) orders her in an undertone to get off at the next stop, while the woman stares at him blankly, not understanding what is wrong. Obediently she leaves the train when it stops, sits down on a bench on the platform, and eventually gets to wherever she was going, stage by stage, still not understanding (since no one has told her) that what is wrong is that she is disgracing a modern cultured nation. And alas the awful fight to get on or off the trains, the collision at the door between those desiring to leave and those desiring to enter, the mild noises of distress from those being trampled underfoot and the mild noises of impersonal deprecation from those doing the trampling – and sometimes the cold cruel foreign voice of someone like myself pointing out loudly that it is illogical for people to suppose they can enter a limited space before other people have vacated it. A proposition which is true, no doubt, but irrelevant, like many another foreign proposition. I hear that these days students are hired by the railways on a part-time basis to push passengers into the carriages by polite brute force. I am rather glad to have been spared this, I doubt I would have been able to endure being shoved, however well-meaningly, by a student who was simultaneously practising his spoken English on me or inquiring after the significance of *The Waste Land*.

And all the people one didn't meet, from whom one received letters, sometimes many and long, and sometimes (one suspected) for all the oddities of expression, extremely intelligent. One might not have held one's own with them for long in a language which they knew well. As it was, one occasionally retired in disorder after a brief interchange which had seemingly begun as fan mail. As in this case:

'Please excuse my prisumption in writing and I couldn't know your name's spelling. I read in the Mainichi-newspaper of last year your lecture about the poem. I think it was very good, and as my English is bad, I shall write briefly.

I have been writing a Japanese poem (Waka), and is very difficult because, as you know, present Japan isn't like old dynasty in which several arts flourished, that of Waka being among them. In those time, people lived with Nature, treating their friends, flowers, birds, breezes, the moon etc. as the ancient Greek people. Japan's poem, the Waka, which is really valuble, was of great use to people of Nara-generations, Heian-generations etc. However present Japan is so different from old. Therefore I have been having difficulties, which are in short – "How to put new wine into old bottles".

We agree with those words of you concerning poetry must be something satisfies the requirements of everybody, that is, every person living in modern world. Therefore present Japan's Waka should contain not only romanticism, classicism, realism, symbolism, nor should be centered round self, but must concern everyone and every everyday things.

Well, Waka's direction which we have taken is progressed to abstract from concrete, namely the inside change to one body of an emotion and making a form. Therefore this direction isn't only classical beauty which already we had. We must have deep observing eyes and deep-personality to make good works. But these are difficult to reach when I'm yet shallow-minded.

Through all ages and western and east, high works of all art are hard to be understood by ordinary people. And so it will be far away from the pleasure which you said. And I like to play piano which I have studied from earnestly my childhood better than writing Waka. However, how are we "to put new wine in old bottles"? If we change the ancient form which is ground on rhythm of the Japanese language, it will not be true Waka.

Recently French poets have been attending to Japanese poetry, its pointblank expression and after the taste. But we, the writers

of Waka, experience hardship if we are to not allow influence
of the complicated modern life to destroy the delicate rhythm
and colour and nuance of Japanese language.

My mistake in this letter is fixed by a Sister of the Convent,
but please excuse my poor letter. If you would be so kind to give
me your ideas, I and my dear Sister would be very happy. I hope
you are healthy.'

The second letter from this correspondent was written on
eight slips of stiffish paper, each in the shape of an open fan,
each sheet a little smaller than the one preceding it and of a
different tint; they were all decorated with varying botanical
forms in silver. At first I took it that the use of this paper, easy
neither to write on nor to read from, was intended as a token
of our growing intimacy. As I read on I could see that it might
rather mark a growing sense of nationalism and a rebuke to
an ignorant busybody of a foreigner.

'I very much appreciate to receive your reply unexpectedly
and for your kind teaching and also I think I must not forget
your courtesy with which you stimulated me.

Then in this letter I have somethings to tell you those are about
poems – present poems from Meiji era to now, that is free verse
you call it – much existing besides Waka. As regards Waka, I
remember a treatise, "Declining Japanese Verse", was introduced in a certain year of Taishō era, happening owing to just
what you mentioned before.

About Waka's 5-syllable-7-syllable, you ask, "Is there any
law of nature which says this is so?" I have to answer, "Yes,
there is." For 5–7 rhythm was born from the limit of natural
utterance of man, is thought therefore to be better than 6 or 9
rhythm.

In present Japanese Waka broken tone is used according to
content and sometimes sour idioms, which was not used in
ancient time, is just as discord in modern music. You say, in
Japan we seem to have only one form. Poetic form is not set
limits to one form. There are lots of forms in Waka like, though
a human body seems to be one shape, really each has his own

style and fully differs in personality, As you say, feeling is combined with form as a noun stop (Waka finished with noun) verb stop (Waka finished with verb) and Syokudome or Sankudome (Waka different between the first phrose and the third phrose in tone or meaning). Of course even in ancient time were many a excellent poet who sang ecstasy, profound agony and life.

I'm afraid you may have a question, But Japanese is so delicate that I can not write all about Waka in English. And so I wish I could talk with you or you to be so good at Japanese like our Missionary.

Tea ceremony as you say has become a genteel pastime, but formerly in the day of Sen-no-Rikyū, it was the philosophy of life. What tea ceremony is, comes from greed of man or especially foolish vanity of woman, Just like even music of Chopin, poetry of piano or soul of piano, is lible to fall into only a saloon music when unskillful young lady including me play it.

Wishing you be in good health and good works.

So long for now.'

And those carefully planned and perfectly executed outings where nothing was left to chance. The blossoms would be opening just as you arrived, the sun (or moon as might be the case) would be in exactly the right position for maximum effect, the car (whose? Often one failed to find out) would be waiting at the station (perhaps it had been waiting since the previous night, like Aziz at the station in Chandrapore?), the famous fish would be posing in their tanks, the saké brewery brewing saké like mad, the monks behaving monkishly, the palace garden looking precisely like its photographs, the sumō champions locked in a long expert embrace, and the restaurant which one happened to come across (just at the right moment) had been on the alert all day, the manageress already at the door in her best kimono and smile . . .

Also the occasional carefully planned treat which chance undid utterly. And never by halves. A gale had blown the blossoms away, the moon was obscured, the fish were dead, the brewery was on strike, the garden closed for the day, the monks gone to an international congress, the wrestling cancelled, the restaurant full ... Like the splendid annual dinner for the trustees of the various establishments forming the educational complex which was crowned by the university where I was employed. This year's dinner was given by (I think) the secondary school for girls, and it was held on the premises, with a first-class Chinese restaurant catering. The trustees were mostly prosperous Osaka businessmen, everyone wore his best dark suit, and my wife was as so often the only woman present. Various trustees of the various establishments made short congratulatory speeches, a fair amount of preliminary drinking had been accomplished and the cold dish was already on the table. Then T-san, who was one of the university trustees, rose ostensibly to add his important voice to this polite and proper chorus. Instead he proceeded to impugn the efficiency of the school trustees, not in respect of the school but in respect of the dinner. He ended, and therewith arose those sad deprecatory noises which (as we had soon come to understand) indicated that something unsuitable had happened close at hand but did not seek to attribute responsibility to anyone present. No finger-pointing, no 'It's his fault', no 'You're drunk, you ought to be ashamed of yourself'. Then they all pushed their chairs back, got to their feet and walked out, thoughtfully, as if they were coming away from the sick-bed of a friend, uncensoriously, but conclusively. 'Come,' said Dr. Jugaku, 'I will take you to a pleasant restaurant in Kobe.' 'But look at all the food!' I protested, sticking fast in my seat, 'It will be wasted! Can't we eat some of it at least?' All those full glasses too. But Dr. Jugaku, our Virgil, shook his head emphatically. 'We must leave.' The occasion was beyond recovery. It must all be as if it had never been. We must not in any way interfere with its non-occurence.

We foreigners were at the best clodhoppers in this context of fine feelings. I felt shamefully gross when a Japanese professor who had specialized in the plays of Christopher Fry (he had written a thesis setting forth in tables the frequency of images of light in Fry and by comparing these with similar tables relating to Shakespeare's plays had proved that Fry was of Shakespearian stature) finally got round to asking me frankly how great I personally considered his favourite author. Honesty, than which few things are more gross, overcame me, and I muttered something to the effect that I doubted whether very much would be heard of Fry in twenty years' time. He was distinctly upset. Some months later I found myself in a Kyoto bar along with Anthony Thwaite (who had recently come to teach in Tokyo) and his wife and this Japanese professor. The other two men were talking together in a corner, when the Japanese turned towards me and said gleefully, 'Ah Mr. Enright, Mr. Thwaite holds that you are mistaken in thinking Christopher Fry will be forgotten in twenty years!' 'Certainly,' put in Anthony Thwaite, 'He'll be forgotten in two years!'

Memories also of a sprinkling of English eccentrics, old Japan hands, their brains addled by long years spent in the country, some of them in detention camps during the war. (But wouldn't their brains have dried up altogether in England?) The old man, now dead, who used to read the news in English on the radio in a splendidly fruity voice, striking dread or astonishment into many a noisy native household. At this time, hardly able to walk, he had dwindled to one sole though inconvenient pleasure – that of being defecated upon by young men. Arrested in a public bath-house once, he was rescued by influential old Japanese friends and protectors, who soothed the alarmed youth and dispersed the bewildered police. Much reference to foreign ways must have come into their explanations, I suspect, and a good deal about respect for old age however foreign. And the middle-aged teacher of English (unsubsidized, not a poet, alas, not a promising young writer, and worst of all a fluent speaker of Japanese) who pulled out his handkerchief at an august gathering of native and foreign diplomats and businessmen, and released a shower of name-cards all with the rounded corners and gilt edges

characteristic of the cards distributed by the inhabitants of
houses of pleasure.

And some visitors who gave as good as they took, like
Benjamin Britten and Peter Pears, at a magnificent dinner
which the Broadcasting Corporation of Japan gave for them
at the Tsuruya, a notable Kyoto teahouse. The most highly-
regarded samisen players and singers were brought in to
entertain the guests. As they performed, Britten scribbled
down the musical notation while Pears (an even greater feat,
I should think) swiftly made his own transliteration of the
words. Then Britten borrowed a samisen and plucked at it
while Pears sang – the result being an uncanny playback. The
effect on the geisha, a race who tend to be excessively conscious of their inimitability, their cultural uniqueness, and
aggravatingly assured of the pitiable inability to understand
their art inherent in all foreigners, was almost alarming. They
paled beneath their whitewash. A more violent people would
have seen to it that their guests' throats were cut the moment
they left those sacred halls. This was one of the few indubitable
triumphs for British art or artists which I noticed in Japan –
and probably the most striking.

Kingsley Martin too – though, as one would expect, a
triumph for British morality in this case – in the lobby of the
expensive Miyako Hotel, also in Kyoto. Mr. Martin was engaged with an art-dealer of some repute who had been
apprised by a third person of Mr. Martin's wish to take back
to England with him some superior examples of the art of the
wood-block print. The art-dealer had arrived with a large
roll of prints under his arm, and I was standing near the entrance watching for the *Asahi* newspaper car which was to
bear the distinguished British journalist to Nara, another
ancient capital. (The British Embassy in Tokyo had called me
earlier to say that Kingsley Martin would be visiting Kyoto,
where they had no representation, and it might be appropriate for me, as an occasional contributor to the back pages
of the *New Statesman*, to meet him. Mr. Martin told me that
since he had implicit trust in his literary editor he hardly

ever looked at the back pages.) I became aware of gasps
coming from Mr. Martin's direction, succeeded by snorts,
and then by a prolonged roar reminiscent of the M.G.M. lion.
The bent figure of the terrified art-dealer scurried past me,
agitatedly rolling up his valuable prints in full flight. And at
once Mr. Martin was at the lobby telephone. 'Is that Mr. X?
Martin here. I cannot imagine what I could possibly have said
last night to give you the impression that I would be interested
in *that* sort of picture . . . Filth, that's what they are, pure filth!'
And down went the telephone. Years later, when a piece I
had written on Nabokov for the *New York Review of Books*
evoked a number of letters from genteel Nabokovians reviling
me for having a dirty mind and being incapable of distinguish-
ing between high art and immorality, I thought enviously of
Kingsley Martin and the fleeing art-dealer and Mr. X. How
well, how expeditiously, he had handled that ancient crux!

And the British Ambassador, an old Japan hand, since he
was born in the country and went to school there, who bravely
and successfully kept his end up even with people who still
remembered him by the unflattering nickname, a cross-
language pun, he had been given at school. One day, in the
course of a duty tour, he was on the point of boarding a pre-
carious-looking cable-car when a hundred or so school children suddenly rushed past him and into the car – a load far in
excess of the prescribed maximum. His Excellency remon-
strated with the man in charge, pointing out among other
things that he was H.B.M. Ambassador travelling on official
business. Apologizing deeply, the conductor yelled at the
children and drove them out of the car. He then bowed the
Ambassador aboard in ceremonious fashion. As His Excellency was expressing his thanks for this courtesy, the conductor beckoned to the children and they all poured back.
The claims of Britain and the necessities of Japan had both
been met.

Humour, even wit, on the part of the conductor? Hard to
be sure. It is particularly difficult to recognize and assess
Japanese humour. At one extreme of course it is easy enough

to detect – the slapstick humour of men in their cups, rarer in occurrence, shorter in duration, but more extreme in degree than elsewhere, and generally more childish, all too relaxed. But the humour of sobriety is largely linguistic, rarefied, abstruse, poetic and hence often rather sad. A friend, a professor, wrote nostalgically to me a year after he had returned from a short trip to England: '"A half of bitter, please" – how sweet it sounds!' There is little to be found between these two extremes, probably because of the concern for 'face': wit at another's expense, however light, is satire, satire is a spoliation of dignity. Oswald Wynd told me that his father, a missionary in Japan, had produced an annotated version of *The Pickwick Papers* for Japanese students with signs in the margin indicating places at which to laugh. This must have saved no end of faces, including Dickens's.

Last but not least of these memories, and no laughing matter, Miss Harada, a victim of the bomb, that great twentieth-century happening, a victim and also a survivor. I hope, still a survivor.

During the first half of my stay in the country, resident foreigners (most of them representatives of foreign companies) were taxed at a lower rate than the Japanese, on the grounds that out of kindliness such foreigners were helping to re-establish a fallen nation. But then, much to the distress of those self-sacrificing foreigners, the Japanese Government abolished this concession on the grounds that Japan was now back on her feet, no longer a defeated and rightly ruined nation. It was about this time that a British Embassy Counsellor, who had worked in Japan for many years before and after the war and spent the interim in an internment camp, was reported to have said with some satisfaction, 'Ah, now they've stopped being polite to me all the time, now they're actually being quite rude. That's better! Now I know where I am.'

One tea-time as we were on our way back to England, the radio in the first-class lounge of the P. & O. ship *Chusan* announced that the Japanese Government had decided to close down Yoshiwara and all other licensed quarters and houses throughout the country. This was received by a long synchronized burst of manic laughter from the male passengers, almost wholly British, who were gathered there. Then came an equally unanimous silence, puzzled, startled and even ashamed. What were we laughing at?

5
What Universities Want

WE had supposed that what we needed at this point was a rest, and that the voyage from Kobe to Tilbury would be restful. It was not notably so. This was the first time I had spent more than ten or twelve days together at sea, and I imagine that it will be the last. I have flown ever since. As the normal horrors of shipboard life are well known to all, except perhaps for those (themselves a minor horror) who at once settle at the best table in the best lounge and play bridge continuously throughout the voyage, I shall not dwell on them. This voyage, which took in several imperial outposts, had its own particular horrors. The ship filled up with *memsahibs* returning to England, with their children but in many cases without the *sahibs*. The *amahs* had been left behind and for the first time for several years mothers were face to face with their offspring, without intermediary, without anywhere to escape to except the ship's bars. There was a 'playground' or lock-up on deck for young children, and a strapping matron to look after them, but we stopped sending our daughter there when we found that, deprived of their loving or long-suffering native nurses, the imperial young turned to something approaching cannibalism. The extreme case was a seven-year-old girl who saw in her mother not so much a stranger as an acknowledged enemy once remote but now suddenly close at hand. The mother's attitude was identical and she spent most of her time in parts of the ship denied to children. This little girl conceived a passionate and violently jealous attachment to my wife. She didn't care much for me, and would order me out of our cabin when she wished to be alone with my wife, as sometimes at night when she turned up in her night-dress ready for bed. I recall getting clawed once; she was very strong. But her special hatred was for our daughter, whom she was once caught in the act of pushing overboard;

she would have succeeded in this had the rail not been just a little too high. How different from the home life of the Japanese, we said to ourselves, already beginning to regret that we hadn't accepted the invitation to stay on for another three years.

I found a small table, set up shop in a comparatively sheltered corner of the deck, and began to type out the final drafts of our translations of modern Japanese poetry. But it seemed that if the only game one was allowed to play on the *Chusan* was bridge, one was not permitted to work at all. Gangs of more or less savage children, who were too big to qualify for the 'playground' or else had been expelled from it for more than usually monstrous behaviour, gathered around me, eager to play rough games with my typewriter, or else in the case of the more sophisticated among them content to point out derisively that they had never heard of a man using a typewriter before and that their daddy in his office in Hong Kong or Singapore had lots of Chinese girls to do that menial work for him. Even adult passengers appeared to find the sight of a grown man sitting at a typewriter very queer indeed, even suspicious, and would pause in their healthful perambulations to tell me so. I felt I had better conceal from them the nature of what I was typing.

But at least we had a roof over our heads and the food was paid for. Once we stepped ashore we would have worse problems to face.

The 'book which we knew of' having put paid to the Egyptian appointment (and I shall unfortunately have more to say about this mystery later), it remained to find another job, and before too long. While on board ship I came across an advertisement for a lectureship or assistant lectureship at the University of the West Indies, and posted off an application at the next port of call. Soon after reaching London, I was called for interview by the Inter-University Council for Higher Education Overseas, a body with which I was to have a fair amount to do in the future, though this first encounter with it was not exactly successful.

The interview took place in the cellar of the Bloomsbury building at that time occupied by the Inter-University Council. The then Professor of English in the West Indies started the ball rolling by remarking amiably that I had written an amusing novel about Egypt – he wasn't to know how painful that pleasantry was – and he rather hoped that if it should happen that I was appointed to this present post I wouldn't find myself inspired to write a comic novel about the West Indies. I was able to reply, with genuine feeling, that I too hoped not. Someone else then asked whether I was intending to engage in any sustained work of research, and while I was endeavouring to find a tactful way of indicating a modest lack of faith in my future as an editor of Middle English texts, the professor, who was genuinely kindhearted, broke in to assure me that the questioner wasn't really inquiring after my research projects but was only worried lest I should be engaged upon work for which the University Library lacked the requisite facilities. But the questioner clearly had no such helpful intention in mind. He was a deceptively benevolent-looking oldish gentleman whose name I cannot divulge because I never found out who he was or in what capacity he sat on the selection board. He then cut across the professor to remark that he noted from my application that while in earlier years I had written literary criticism, it would appear that of late I had published nothing but poems and a novel. Why was that? In fact I had published a decent amount of criticism lately, in fact I had a collection of critical essays in the press at that moment, but I took his question seriously and replied that I had the feeling that rather too much literary criticism was coming out and it might be as well if some of us free-wheeled for a while. This soft answer failed to turn away the old gentleman's wrath. 'Poems and novels are all very well,' he declared, 'all very well, but what a university wants is *literary criticism*. Literary criticism – *that* is what a university wants!'

It was my turn to grow annoyed, for the professor had already warned me that though the post had been advertised as a lectureship or assistant lectureship it now appeared that most probably there would be funds sufficient only for an appointment at assistant lecturer level. I had in turn intimated that even so I was still interested. No doubt it would be a sad falling-off, from visiting professor to assistant lecturer, the lowest rung on the academic ladder, but I was deficient in academic ambition and I felt that the reputedly cheerful extroverts of the West Indies were just what we needed after the tragic and introverted Japanese. Moreover, what we needed was a job. But all the same the West Indies could hardly expect to procure a combination of Leavis, Skeat and Matthew Arnold for a miserable assistant lectureship. The interview ended in an atmosphere of constraint, and in due course I was informed that I had not been selected for the post.

It was now that the British Council (for whom I had done occasional chores in Japan) came to the rescue. Presumably they didn't want literary criticism. It would be difficult to say what they did want. I was called to Davies Street and appeared before a rather large board, and sitting on that board (somehow I wasn't surprised: in Japan one had been spoilt in one sense, now one was to be spoilt in another) was the doubtfully benevolent old gentleman with a lust for literary criticism. But this time he did not intervene; he merely nodded at me in a not unkindly though knowing way. The post for which the board was selecting was at the Free University in West Berlin, and someone asked whether my wife, as a Frenchwoman, would be happy living in Germany. I didn't really think she would be, but I knew she would be even less happy living out of a couple of suit-cases in a room in a London hotel. Misgivings were stifled on both sides, and shortly afterwards we went to Berlin.

6

Berlin

When the man
Was dragged out from under
The debris
Of his shelled house,
He shook himself
And said:
Never again.

At least, not right away.

GÜNTER KUNERT
trans. MICHAEL HAMBURGER

WE arrived in Berlin two months after Bertolt Brecht died. I look back on the ten months I spent there as the quietest time of that part of my life under recall here, and probably the least rewarding. One learnt of course what 'cold war' meant, but the lesson was dull and deadening. Friends told us that we were going to live in a most exciting place at a most significant time. In practice it turned out to be about as exciting as Leamington Spa in the days of my youth.

In some respects the atmosphere was strangely similar. However different the cause, there was the same intense and petty concern for gentility, the same habit of judging people by their most external manifestations, the same sense of being stifled mentally and emotionally. Some part of this impression of mine must have derived from purely personal circumstances. For something had gone wrong along the line between Davies Street and Dahlem. Since I was under contract to the British Council I qualified for a sort of associate membership of Allied Forces (British) Berlin, and to begin with the Free University showed itself somewhat hostile, regarding me as an academic nobody whom for reasons yet to emerge British Military Government was interested in foisting upon them in collusion with the British Council. The war had been over for some time, and naturally the university preferred to choose its own staff. In the eyes of British Military Government I was equally dubious, though in other ways. I was frowned upon for wearing a sports jacket instead of a dark suit (German academics wore dark suits, and I ought to conform) and for not owning a car (German academics didn't usually run cars, and as a representative of the victorious side I ought to demonstrate superiority by not conforming). There were other sources of dissatisfaction (yes, just like Leamington Spa!). On the British side: my hair was too long, I was a lover of peace and a person of liberal tendencies, apolitical and therefore Leftist. On the German side: I was a journalist, the lowest form of literate life, I had just come from Japan (far indeed from the home where the Beowulf roams), and I was proposing to teach 'neuere Literatur'. So this was Berlin.*

In the West, the garish frontage of the Kurfürstendamm, that long shop window of shop windows, with its *konditorei*, eating-houses equipped with 'vomitoria' (roomy latrines sporting sturdy handrails) and free second helpings, bars, cinemas, theatres, sausages, cream cakes, stout ladies and well-kept dogs, and men who resembled the vulgar English conception of Germans. In the East, the untidy and ubiquitous ruins, or rubble rather, which seemed to have been

---

* I would like to speak very earnestly to the reader at this point. More than once during the writing of these memoirs I have dropped my pen in acute embarrassment. Would anyone *believe* what I had written? Would it not appear that I was making up stories, that I was being malicious – in a remarkably childish fashion? I can only beg the reader to believe that if I were making up stories intended to defame, discredit or bring into contempt, then I would take care to make them more 'credible', more malicious, and considerably more self-flattering than these poor little truths are. Falstaff was not only witty in himself but also the cause that wit was in other men. On this analogy, my stupidity must be of generous proportions, for I have certainly been the cause of notable stupidity in other men.

left there deliberately as a symbol of moral superiority, to offset the inferiority of Communist sausages and cakes. Poor but honest. And then, as if to accentuate the ruins, the Hollywood set of Stalin-Allee, still rather poor, but with a dishonest expression on its large stony face.

In the West, a bar called 'Cherchez la Femme', where I once went with an English friend. The huge uniformed commissionaire, who was walking to and fro on the pavement clashing his fists together to keep warm, sought to discourage us from entering. *'Kein Bier hier, meine Herrn!'* waving us down the street to some more suitable *lokal*, 'No beer, no beer!' So what, we answered, we should drink wine then, did he think that Engländer were only good enough for beer? We stood on our rights, and he let us in reluctantly. The bar was empty of customers, but full of splendidly-bosomed young ladies who appeared to be there not to entertain the clientele but to entertain one another. I offered the mythological blonde behind the counter a high-class English cigarette (from the Naafi), and she took it after several disdainful refusals. Two disgusted puffs, and she crushed it savagely in the ashtray. We were a long way away from the days when a packet of Senior Service would have bought a whole cabaret-full of girls. A little later I was sharply rebuked for interfering with a candle by trying to light my pipe from it: it was strongly forbidden to spill grease on the table. We gulped down our rather expensive bottle of cheap wine and slunk out. No beer – sneered the commissionaire – you see! Beer down the street, my sirs! In retrospect it could be seen that the commissionaire's intentions were in part friendly and he may even have been speaking in a sort of code, for we later found that 'Cherchez la Femme' was reputed to be a Lesbian hangout. On the other hand, I remember a small dim bar on Kant-strasse in which I was charged double price for a bottle of wine because I had brought my wife. Presumably this was a heterosexual hangout.

In the East, the well-appointed restaurant on Stalin-Allee,

where aristocratic-looking Hungarian officers were con-
suming aristocratic-looking dishes, and we were required to
produce our identity cards, whereupon we were warned
that our East-marks (procured at three to one West-mark)
would not be accepted and we would have to pay in West-
marks at par. And so, like bewildered peasants just up from
the village, we could only afford a small fried egg without
garnishings. And May Day in the East, with crowds of
workers preparing to parade round Marx-Engels-Platz (a
spot earlier known as the Lustgarten). At the marshalling
points beery men were embracing their wives and sweet-
hearts, filling the air with such loud bucolic bussings and
hearty cries of valediction that one would have thought they
were about to march off to the front.

In Berlin the choice seemed to be between genuine
boredom and factitious excitement.

So uncertain was my status at the Free University that I
was given little to do, and nothing of any curricular importance. Attendance at my classes was purely voluntary so
that, though I had few students, I had some of the very best.
For me they redeemed Berlin. That today a high proportion
of them are living outside Germany, in America, Sweden,
the East, has nothing to do with my unsettling influence.
They were aware that for a profitable academic career
intelligence and sensitivity would serve them less well than
prudent conformism and an attitude of measured servility
towards their professorial seniors. I was chatting once with a
student, a clever, rather over-earnest girl who had spent
some time at Trinity College, Dublin, when the head of the
English Department walked past. To my amazement, and
to her own, she dropped him a formal curtsy, the first I
had ever seen outside a theatre. 'I didn't mean to,' she
lamented, 'I couldn't help myself!' I understood, I almost
couldn't help myself either.

But if relations between staff and students were distant and
slight, relations within the staff, between lower and higher
grades, were hardly more intimate. In Germany, or so my

brief experience suggested, an ordinarius is a mighty god –
and gods don't make the best teachers. The Free University
(its name affiliates it rather unfortunately with the Free
World's shop window on the Ku'damm) was at least free
from Communism and so drew many students across from
East Berlin and the old Friedrich-Wilhelm (now Humboldt)
University. I didn't notice that it was notably free in other
ways. Possibly the livelier academics at this time were still
over in East Berlin – and in trouble or about to be. But the
only Eastern academics I met were a seedy Scot, who gave
the appearance of having held on to his Communist faith
through sheer miserliness, and a sinister German. The two
of them used to circulate freely in West Berlin, visiting the
British Centre from time to time to collect old newspapers
and back numbers of English magazines, ostensibly for use
in their English classes, though some people thought the
real reason was to prevent these periodicals falling into
unauthorized hands.

One of my small band of students, a sensitive or over-
sensitive and highly-strung girl who wrote poetry, stayed
in Germany and spent the next ten years being a scholar,
a literary scientist in the best German manner. She gave
herself, as she put it, to the study of the thesis of Professor A
(deriving from the thesis of Professor B on 'The figurative
meaning of worm metaphors in the North-Thuringian
imitations of *Heautontimoroumenos*', 1861, p. 759) presented
in rebuttal of the thesis of Professor C (in turn based on the
thesis of Professor D, 'The worm in middle high German
elegy', 1897, footnote 393) and contending that the worm
mentioned in Konrad von Fussesbrunnen, *Kindheit Fest*,
1.5183), was male rather than female. Now, 'booksy and
erudite, having lost so much time, I have to creep back to
the sources of my former talent', if only she can find them.
She is writing short stories, and not surprisingly they always
come out as satires on German university life.

.   .   .   .   .

The bad public behaviour of the Japanese had often disturbed and angered us. The good public behaviour of the Germans, compared with whom the British are a rabble of hysterical dagoes, I found more acutely alarming. Disorder along with charm is feasible; order accompanied by politeness is highly acceptable. But order along with a stupid uncouthness is intolerable. On one occasion in a post office I took up position to the left of the person being served, as there were but the two of us. Then others joined at his right and were served one after another, while I was completely ignored. Eventually quite a long queue had formed, and I sought to explain that it was my turn to be dealt with, indeed long past my turn, but the newcomers therewith turned upon me and informed me with heartfelt indignation and outrage that queues were invariably formed to the right and since I was standing to the left of centre I could not be said to have any official existence. I know I sound very petty; but petty was how I found Berlin much of the time. Perhaps it was the price of being the powder-barrel of the world.

Rather more painful to witness was the embarrassment of some British officials and officers when in the company of middle-aged German males. It would be pointed out to them that they too had queued on the wrong side, they had fought and worse defeated their obvious ally, Germany, thus enabling the obvious enemy, Russia, to pluck the fruits in comfort. They had been proleptic traitors, so to speak, to the Free World which was around the corner. What could the British do, but drop their eyes in shame? For now they were not occupying but defending, and it wouldn't have done, in West Berlin, to drag up that prehistoric Hitler. Only the young might talk of Hitler, with them it was a solecism such as may be expected from the young; with the grown-ups it smacked of treason.

'The truth is concrete': this was Brecht's slogan. There did not appear to be much in Berlin in 1956 and 1957 that was concrete, apart from the new buildings and the old ruins.

One had the feeling that real life, or real death, was going on somewhere else. We often had recourse to a recording we had bought of Lotte Lenya singing Kurt Weill's songs, some of them settings of poems by Brecht: there seemed to be more of Berlin on that disc than was to be found outside. But there were, for me, a few students, clear-eyed and therefore wrinkled of brow, and one or two of the more junior of my colleagues on the teaching staff. There was Frau L—, our *Putzfrau*, a cheerful sturdy girl who came over from East Berlin twice a week to set the flat in order and spend her earnings on the better-quality clothing and footwear available in the West. Her political views were confined to a stoical regretfulness over the excessive number of parades her hard-working husband had to turn out for. She was the friendliest of the Germans we met. Later, when we were in Bangkok, she wrote to us in the painfully careful hand of one not accustomed to the practice, a gentle stoical letter, hoping that the weather was not too hot for our comfort and that we found the native people well disposed.

We were fortunate, too, in that our stay coincided with that of Francis Golffing and his wife Barbara Gibbs, both of them poets. Francis had taken a year off from Bennington College to teach in the Department of American Literature at the Free University. This pair, to whom we had been introduced by Marius Bewley, shone out like large luminaries of civilization in that weird twilight; they did not believe that only a dead hand could do battle successfully with another dead hand, or that the way to preserve a degree of freedom was to put the whole of it into long-term pickle. And one of the high-lights of our year was a visit by John Willett, then researching for his book on Brecht's theatre. He took us to the stage canteen at the Theater am Schiffbauerdamm, where we met some of the members of the Berliner Ensemble. They didn't strike me as a notably 'political' set of people; their attitude seemed similar to Brecht's as described in Martin Esslin's book on him, except somewhat disheartened. Perhaps they did not share the

master's relish for tightrope walking. Yet was there for
them, with their necessities, their history and their loyalties,
anywhere distinctly better to go? Where was there a better
hole, a better theatre? Their founder, on the run from Hitler,
hadn't managed too brilliantly in America, for all his canni-
ness. 'When they accused me of wanting to steal the Empire
State Building, I thought it was high time for me to leave.'

I tried in a number of poems to capture the atmosphere of
Berlin – the divided city and its choice of unattractions, and
above all that stony division of people from people of which
the later Wall was merely a simple and calamitously apt
symbol – or tried to capture my impressions of its atmosphere. But most of what I produced would hardly strike
the reader as other than perversely petulant – why on earth
all these complaints about the efficiency of the refuse-disposal
services or the German fondness for dogs? – or else incomprehensible. All the poems in the world couldn't put Berlin
together again. Barbara Gibbs did better when she quite
simply described Berlin as

> a city rotted like an old lace curtain
> Where someone has spilled drops of vitriol.

A few drops had spattered on the façade of the apartment
house in which after considerable difficulty we had found a
lodging. The address was by far the best thing about it:
Goethe-strasse. The flat itself, with too much heavy furniture in too small a space, with grossly cheery and untrue
Bavarian poker-work mottoes and masses of china figurines
which combined the minimum grace with the maximum
accumulation of dirt and couldn't be cleaned without being
broken – the flat itself certainly corresponded to the common
British misconception of that great German. Goethe-strasse
is in the Charlottenburg district, close to the Ku'damm and
Kant-strasse, not far from the Zoo, five stops away from
Marx-Engels-Platz on the S-Bahn. At the end of Goethe-

strasse was (and I hope still is) Steinplatz, the epitome of
Berlin for me, with its neat lawn and its two little well-
balanced memorial tablets, one in memory of those killed
by Hitlerism, the other in memory of those killed by
Stalinism. Almost everyday I would repair there, and

> shuffle through the little park,
>   from stone to stone,
> From conscience-cancelling stone to stone,
> Peering at the fading ribbons on the faded wreaths.

It was, I thought, an eminently well-named place.

Our landlady was of the true line of Berlin landladies, a
ferocious and much-feared race. Some of them were pitiable,
middle-aged war widows obliged to break up their comfortable *bourgeois* establishments into bed-sitting rooms and
take in persons they wouldn't have been seen dead with in
the good old days. The students had many stories of landladies who offered free accommodation against payment in
kindness; generally students preferred to pay in coin, however hard up they were, because (they said) the other way
interfered with their work too much. The Golffings' landlady, an old lady, suffered from insomnia and would often
come into their bedroom in the small hours, wake them
up and sit down at the foot of the bed for a nice long
chat.

Though our landlady was a widow of sorts, she was not
noticeably pitiable. Her husband had done a bunk, by a
strange coincidence he had (she told us) run away all the way
to Japan. She was a formidable piece of womanhood, short
but capacious, two-thirds bust and one-third backside, a
lover of whisky (mine, ex-Naafi) and of cream cakes and
other goodies. And also of money. The housing situation in
Berlin was extremely bad, and we (or rather the British
Council) were prepared to pay a handsome rent. Besides
kitchen and bathroom, the flat appeared to consist of only
one largish room, but the landlady ripped away a strip of
wallpaper and revealed a second room, rather small, in

which cowered two frightened white-faced little people. This unhappy pair were chased out in short order, and the landlady willingly banished herself to her sister's establishment in Schleswig-Holstein, having first accepted several months' rent in advance and instructed us that I was to sleep on the couch in the small room while my wife and daughter occupied the bed-settee in the larger one. We then moved in, into what space was available between the radio-gram, the piano (alas useless to us) and the elephantine chairs and tables. We took down some of the more distressing pictures and proverbs and packed the figurines and statuettes, shepherds, shepherdesses and other wild life, into a cupboard where they contrived to do damage to one another.

As a change from the oppressive furnishings of the flat and the stony strangulation of the city we planned to go away for a week at Easter, and for some odd reason we booked in at an hotel on a mountain-top in Carinthia. It appeared that at this time the ski-ing would be all over and the snow safely melted away into the green carpet of mother earth – I suppose we thought the air would be good for the child.

Had I been a layman I would merely have needed to obtain a visa from the East German authorities and we could then have taken a long-distance coach through 'the zone'. Had I been in receipt of full logistic support from British Military Government we could have travelled in the sealed military train which left every night for Hanover. As it was, since Britain did not recognize the East German state, British Military Government would have to ask the Russians to grant a visa. If at the time relations were coldly peaceful, the Russians would oblige. If relations were coldly hostile, they would ask in a nasty way – Why do you come to us? If you want a visa for travel through the German Democratic Republic then address yourselves to the appropriate authorities of the Democratic Republic! In our case the latter happened, so we had to fly out.

Something had gone amiss with the weather forecast, and we found the snow in a disagreeable state of thaw, unsuitable for ski-ing but also for walking. We resigned ourselves to more claustrophobia in the hotel – we *had* made a firm booking – when suddenly the management announced that it intended to close and the last cable-car would be leaving for the flatland in a matter of hours. This unexpected release enabled us to spend a few days very enjoyably in Salzburg.

In the meanwhile the British Council had fixed me up with a new contract and a new posting, to Bangkok. In order to spend some time with her parents in France, my wife left Berlin, along with the child, several weeks ahead of me. They had been gone only three or four days when the doorbell rang and I found the landlady beaming on the step, in full feather, with a mass of suitcases being dropped at her feet by a taxi-driver. She explained that a kind neighbour had written to tell her that my family had departed, and since I was all alone I obviously wouldn't need the whole of her large apartment to myself, and therefore she had hastened thither from Schleswig-Holstein at the earliest opportunity. The suggestion was that she was doing me a considerable favour, which made it the harder for me to remind her that the flat was still mine since the rent had been paid up to and indeed beyond the future date of my departure. (No call for kindness here!) We got bogged down in a rather complex argument, difficult for me to sustain either gracefully or forcibly with my limited vocabulary in German, revolving about the concepts of Need (I didn't need the whole of this large apartment) and Want (I wanted the whole of this flat). But at least while she was talking she wasn't unpacking her bags. She burst out with a contemptuous assurance that I needn't be afraid that she would –

I forgot the German expression she used, though I can remember the coarseness with which she invested it – interfere with me. I had a brief poignant vision of her 'Mann' being interfered with exquisitely by a bevy of soft-voiced slim geisha in a magnificently under-furnished tea-house. I stood my ground: the rent was in her bank, therefore the flat was mine. She turned nasty, or nastier, and began peering and poking about for signs of damage to her property. The scratches on the table, I pointed out, were mostly of ancient origin, possibly caused by shrapnel, but I offered to pay for the figurine of a goose in flight which had lost half an inch of its bill. . . . Finally I threatened to call in the police. This, though abject, did the trick. Five minutes later she was down in the street, with me slung about with her cases (one of them now containing a bottle of Naafi whisky) and hunting for a taxi. Off she was borne, to some other unfortunate sister, leaving me a free man. Incredulously free! For once I found myself blessing the police, and the deep respect in which Germans hold them. Even so, I took to bolting the door at nights.

It was soon time to go, after my one small victory. I had accomplished little in Berlin, aside from preserving my inconsiderable virtue against a landlady. Even my first (and last) attempt to write an occasional poem miscarried. The British Centre had acquired new premises which were to be opened formally by a British general, and I was invited (indeed it was time I did something to earn my British bread) to compose some appropriate verses for inclusion in the souvenir programme. Notwithstanding a rhyme scheme of (for me) unheard-of strictness, and despite the cunning introduction of a line in *echt Deutsch* from Goethe's *Faust,* my poem was found unusable. It was undeniably a feeble piece of poetry, but worse, it contained a message to the effect that literature was an empire with no seat of government, continuous and thus independent of national and political frontiers – a notion as little acceptable to the authorities in West Berlin as it would have been in the East. It had come

to be felt in the vicinity of British Military Government and
its ancillary limbs, I gathered, that I would do better in the
Far East, where politics were thought to be less omnipresent
than in stern old Europe.

As I sank in the estimation of my compatriots, so I rose in
that of my German colleagues. It had at least become plain
that I was not an agent of British Military Government or
the perfidious Foreign Office. During my last weeks there,
the Free University proposed that I should come over to
them on an extended appointment, but by then I had already
agreed to go to Thailand, and I too suspected (not altogether
accurately) that I would do better in the Far East. I must add
here that, some twenty-one months later, after leaving
Bangkok in rather peculiar circumstances, I was offered
an extraordinary professorship at the Free University.
While an extraordinary professorship is less extraordinary
than an ordinary professorship, this was an extraordinarily
generous offer, and though I felt obliged to decline it, all the
more heartening for coming at a time of considerable (but I
hope well-concealed) personal distress.

E

7
Literary London

FOR the first time in our lives I had found a new job before giving up the old one. The break between leaving Berlin and flying to Bangkok was a real holiday, even a holiday with pay. To begin with I spent a few days in London with a friend who had married recently. One evening, together with another old Japan hand and his wife, we dined out at one of London's less satisfactory Chinese restaurants, were requested to leave a pub for humming an English folksong under our breath, and adjourned to the Mandrake Club. It was the first time I had entered this celebrated institution – and, again, probably the last. My friend had been very friendly with a West Indian nurse before his marriage – the West Indies form a tenuous but lengthy thread in these memoirs – and on hearing of his intention to take a wife she had told him that, should they ever meet, she would scratch out her supplanter's eyes. And, my friend told me, she would at that, she was a passionate, primitive creature. As we descended a flight of sinister stairs into the club my friend remarked on how funny it would be if Grace should happen to be there. Yes, it would, said I, and we both laughed masculinely.

As I was gazing about me nervously – in Egypt I had contracted the habit of at once locating possible storm centres and also quick exits – I heard my friend saying rather loudly, 'Hello, Grace, fancy seeing you here! . . . I did tell you I was getting married, didn't I? You must meet my wife.' Grace, a large and powerfully-built and distinctly West Indian lady, shook hands quite nicely, and the rest of us were introduced. My friend, whose talent for unearned imperturbability I had long had cause to resent, disappeared to get the drinks. Grace watched my friend's wife – I omit the obvious simile, though it was altogether apt – and I watched Grace. The graciousness was fast waning, and I remembered what my friend had said about her violent disposition. He had also given me the impression that Grace was a considerable beauty, which I couldn't agree with personally, but I felt, from the look in her eyes that he had been correct as regards the violence. I yearned for those tiny bars, squeezed between brothels in Kyoto and Kobe, their gentlemanly habitués, ladylike ladies and tame playful rats. 'You're alone,' my friend then told me briskly, 'You'd better keep her happy.'

His wife, a well-bred English girl, would not have lasted five seconds against Grace. I thought of her poor, mild, slightly myopic eyes. She was after all my kind hostess. So I took Grace away to dance. I cannot recall how the conversation went, or whether there was any, apart from one declaration of hers. 'He and I are married in the eyes of God,' she said in a husky and convinced voice. I replied rather fearfully that I could understand how she felt, but God was sometimes a bit short-sighted. Fortunately she did not seem to be of a specially religious cast of mind and took no offence. In a rather unenthusiastic way she sought to introduce me to her friends, a seated row of five or six sturdy male West Indians, who were regarding me stonily. But wishing to keep the number of potential combatants to a minimum, I cried gaily, 'On with the dance!'

A little later she excused herself, to dance with one of the men she was presumably with. It struck me as most unfair that what happened next should have happened just at that moment, in that context of painful altruism. My friend (he was the friend of too many people, it appeared) came up leading someone he had known at college, a poet of repute who (as I was aware) had recently spent some time as a visiting professor at my old university in Alexandria. My friend was sure that we would like to meet each other. Certainly I looked forward to news of Alexandria, but the poet, having taken in the identity of the person he was being brought to meet, cast down my hand as if it were a scorpion and roared in fury, 'Ha! You thought you were coming back to Egypt! It was I – I – it was I who stopped you! You wrote a bad – a *bad* book – about Egypt! I took it to them, I made them read it. I wasn't going to have you coming back. Cruel, bad book, about the Egyptians. . . . I'm glad I stopped you. . . .'

He was buffeting me inexpertly about the chest and shoulders, and I was swaying backwards and forwards like a lead-weighted toy at the limits of its performance. The grounds of his dissatisfaction with me shifted slightly – ah these literary pubs! – 'No one can write novels *and* poetry! No one. You think you can write novels *and* poetry. Nobody on this earth can write novels *and* poems. . . .'

'D. H. Lawrence?' I proposed timidly, 'Thomas Hardy? George Meredith?' I tried hard to keep the peace, content with suggesting that even if in fact it was impossible for the same person to write both novels and poems – and I would grant that he had an interesting point there – it was still not unlawful, it was not a capital crime, to *attempt* to write both, one could but try. It was clear, though, that before very long I was going to have to hit him back. I was loth to do this, partly out of a natural aversion to the use of brute force, partly because the poet was partially blind as well as drunk. As I struggled with the morals of the situation, my chastiser suddenly ceased beating his fists against my upper body, dropped his arms to his sides, looked slightly confused, and said in a not unamiable tone, 'I must go for a piss.' And off he went.

He didn't return from the lavatory, or at all events I didn't see him again. I was not displeased with the peaceful conclusion to the episode, and distinctly gratified to have discovered the solution to the mystery of *le livre que vous savez*. It had seemed unlikely to me that the Egyptians, a people extremely tolerant towards the lapses of foreigners, would have taken strong objection to a mere novel. Unless someone had obliged them to do so as a matter of honour.

Though the poet didn't come back, Grace did. Her earlier

urbanity had vanished altogether, and I began to feel that a large part of her anger with my friend's wife was transferring itself to me as being an insufficient surrogate for my friend. Not only was Grace not (in my eyes) a dusky belle, she was coming to seem discernibly ill-favoured. I was feeling weary. It had been an unnaturally long evening. I was looking forward to bed. But I had to keep Grace occupied, if not satisfied, while over at the far end of this dreadful place my friend was dancing with the woman who was his wife in the eyes of men. And I became distressfully aware that somehow or other it had been agreed between us, though without my volition, that I should go off with Grace. To her room, I much feared. It was very near closing time, and I noticed my good friends mounting the stairs into a better world. Grace went aside to reclaim her handbag, left in the care of her compatriots. I shook off her hand. 'I'll wait here for you,' I said, simulating without difficulty fear of jealous assault by her friends. I waited as long as I dared and then sprang up the stairs, reaching the street just as my friends were stepping into a taxi. 'Oh, so you're coming with us?' my friend remarked commiseratingly as I leapt in, 'Too bad you didn't make out with Grace. She's terrific in bed.'

Afterwards I wished I had remembered to thank the poet for having saved us from going to Egypt just in time for the Suez débâcle. As it was, in Berlin I had merely had to observe my more loyal British colleagues striving to justify their Government's behaviour against the outraged protests of the young Germans they were supposed to be civilizing.

8

Bangkok

NOVEMBER 1957. It was good to be back in the East, even though for a while we caught ourselves addressing taxi-drivers in bad German to start off with and then in bad Japanese. And the Thais, we were going to realize, were as different from the Japanese as they were from the Germans. We were lucky enough to find a splendid house, a large open structure standing in a sizeable garden or compound. More correctly, the house was found for us by the wife of my chief, the British Council Representative in Bangkok. The fact that it stood almost directly opposite a brothel escaped her notice, as it escaped ours too for almost a year. The brothel was a respectable establishment, not given to advertising its wares, and, moreover, at this time the new-fangled 'massage parlours', 'Turkish baths' and 'cabaret dance-halls' were all the rage (they would even provide you with a massage or a bath or a dance if necessary) and consequently business had slumped in the old-style houses. Later on in a fit of morality Marshal Sarit was to close down most of the massage parlours and set huge padlocks on the doors of the dance-halls, thus diverting the flood of trade back to our neighbours. This led to a sad incident which I shall leave till the end of the chapter since that is indeed what it amounted to. At the time of which I am writing we were vaguely conscious of an indeterminate number of young ladies coming and going in the compound across the way, and we supposed them to be daughters, nieces, friends or servants of the house. They kept to themselves, their visitors were few and well-behaved; peace, quiet and order prevailed in our lane, a cul-de-sac terminating in a factory which made cheap furniture. It was our landlord who enlightened us, describing the place as an establishment of a quite superior order, so much so (he said)

that it was somewhat akin to a club, and patrons could take
out season tickets.

I am sorry to begin this section of my memoirs on such a
note. I am even sorrier that the truth will oblige me to end
it on a similar though shriller one. But the reader should
kindly refrain from anticipating.

My official designation was British Council Professor of
English at Chulalongkorn University. My duties and
responsibilities were considerably less grand. The post was,
or could have been, a comfortable one, for it involved none
of the administrative and representational work which
takes up so much more of a professor's time and energy
and so much less of his intelligence and effort than teaching
does. The British Council Professor was in reality a free-gift
teacher, and the governance of the department remained
firmly in Thai hands. I for one never felt the slightest inclination to try to wrest it from those hands. The only chore
outside teaching that came my way, as I recall, was to sit on
a small committee of teachers appointed to rationalize the
syllabus, a syllabus which bore even less relation to the
realities of the classroom than syllabuses commonly do. It
seemed unlikely, to say the least, that anyone was seriously
attempting to teach Sartre to young people whose French
was minimal and who were well contented with a simplistic
but comprehensive form of Buddhism. We drew up our
proposals and were about to present them to a gathering of
our colleagues when the Dean of the Faculty, obviously in a
pet, strode into the room and announced that no changes
could possibly be made to the syllabus because firstly the
Ministry of Education did not want any and secondly if we
started tampering with syllabuses then American universities
might well withdraw the recognition they accorded to our
degrees. Hence there was no need for the present meeting,
and so, good morning, gentlemen.

One felt some irritation, but only briefly. It was difficult to sustain resentment for long in Thailand: a light, fragrant, mollifying oil flowed over everything. Smiles, graceful salutations, neatness, clean linen, gentle jokes, prettiness . . . there could be nothing seriously amiss in such a land. Even when – and this was rare for I can remember only one instance – a student happened to let drop in private that an uncle or remoter relative had disappeared, either picked up on suspicion of improper political attitudes or slipped underground to avoid arrest, the conversation sounded like idle chatter about an acquaintance who had gone into hospital for an appendectomy.

One of my British colleagues teaching English language in another faculty used to visit several of his students who had been put in prison without trial. Before long he had a visit himself, from the police. Sweetly, incredulously, they reasoned with him: 'Why should a gentleman like you be interested in such people?' Until recently he was general secretary of the International Secretariat of Amnesty International. Bangkok, in its small and quiet way, with that public gentility which private deafness and blindness make possible, could have provided him with an illustration of how easy it is for people to vanish, without fuss, leaving apparently no trace of their existence, utterly unremarked. No doubt many detainees, in this country and in others, re-emerge later on and take up a normal life, but that they do so is more often due to the clemency or the whim of the régime than to public concern. I once heard a British diplomat chiding a senior Thai official for his government's leniency towards a handful of Thai students who had just returned from a university in China: the government had decided not to imprison the students until they did something. I thought then (as I have thought on several other occasions, but prudence so far has won the day) of turning in my British passport. Even a mendicant mercenary has some dim vestigial sense of patriotism to be hurt.

9

Thai Personalities

The errors of a wise man make your rule,
Rather than the perfections of a fool.

BLAKE

NOT long ago I had occasion to examine an earnest
study of Thai peasant personality, or more precisely, or
lengthily, a study of the patterning of interpersonal behaviour
in a certain Thai village. The author derived much of his
basic data from the responses of a number of peasants to a
test requiring the completion of various sentences, or (as the
author himself put it) to 'a series of standardized stimuli'.
One of the set sentences was 'When something worries
him, he . . .' and this sentence was completed by nearly
half of the selected villagers with a phrase signifying 'felt
worried'. Another sentence ran 'The thing which we want
the most is. . . .', and this sentence seventy-seven per cent
of the villagers completed economically with the word
'money'. By the end of the book, after careful tabulation
and analysis, a lot of terminological expertise or jargon,
and twenty-two months of 'field research' in the village,
the author had arrived at various sensible and largely just
conclusions concerning the salient features of Thai personality and behaviour which would have occurred to an
intelligent and active tourist within his first week of sojourn
in the country.

Since the practice of studying human beings as simple
animals or as animals amenable to simple analysis at the
hands of specialists has now been accorded the status of an
academic subject (and after all, given that both the world
and the academic profession are over-populated, it is true
there is no time for complexity), I feel emboldened to em-
ploy here an even simpler technique for the exploration of

Thai personality. This technique is based on the analysis of students' howlers and pseudo-howlers, and since the latter all derive from one year's crop of examination scripts marked by me personally, I cannot be accused of undue selectiveness.

More than is the case with other student-races using English as a foreign language, the 'mistakes' of the Thais have struck me as handsomely consistent or 'pattern-making' and significant in fairly directly confirming their attitudes and behaviour as observed in other spheres. It will be gathered from the report that I do not altogether subscribe to the theory which holds the Thais to be a simple, innocent, cheerful, outgoing and somewhat backward people (this last adjective generally implies the attached adverb 'conveniently'). Whereas the external demeanour of the Japanese seems calculated to induce outsiders to consider them more extraordinary and incomprehensible than they are, the demeanour of the Thais impresses me as calculated to persuade outsiders that they are more ordinary and easily understood than they are. As I say, the specimens which follow have not been painstakingly culled over a period of years: they all fell in the same seasonal and local shower. And while students of every nationality and race produce howlers (if only to entertain their teachers), I believe that these particular ones could not, with a few exceptions, derive from Japanese, Egyptian, Indian, Singaporean, Malaysian or Chinese students.

'If the poet always sings the truth, he would have a little raw material to produce his work because there are not much truths.'

'Poetry makes the world, the nature, have more technique colours than it really was.'

'If men study poetry which is too romantic, it may lead to sadness at the end.'

'"Fear no more the heat o' the sun" means: now we have air-conditioning.'

These wise comments indicate the realism of the Thais, their only mildly regretful acceptance of things-as-they-are. It is not so much a cynical or pessimistic attitude as a Buddhistically modest view of this world of dew, this world of small expectations. We note too the direct and common-sense interpretation of literary texts (and an honest un-Luddite appreciation of the blessings of progress which ought to touch the heart of Sir Charles Snow). The strong disinclination for flights of fancy, the willingness to suppose that what the poet means is what he most obviously says (even though it is wrong), this is very different from the ingenious profundity evinced by Japanese students of literature, whose respect for poetry is so immense that it sometimes leads them to ignore the poem. There are not many truths in the world, and the Thai is in happy but not arrogant possession of the most important of them. Western writers, and poets in particular, make a great song and dance about all sorts of funny fabricated pseudo-truths, far-fetched imaginings and sensational postulations, but all this adds up to little more than technicoloring and will lead to sadness (if to nothing worse) in the end. The penny-plain sort of truth is what counts. The first of my specimens, incidentally, is near to the description of Freud by a Western-trained Thai psychiatrist reported in the study of Thai peasant personality already mentioned: 'a person who did not have too much to say because he wrote only about sex.'

'R. Greene wrote "A Groansworth of Wit".'

'Shakespeare was the great oppressive figure in Elizabethan period.'

'A ballad usually consists of four lines and jealousy.'

'Alliteration means making of literature all the time.'

'Dr. Prime Rose ... a character in "The Vigor of Wakefield".'

'In rhyme there are both eternal and external rhymes.'

Again we observe a sober and realistic estimation of literature's importance, especially as compared with the genuine verities – Buddhism, the Monarchy, food, rest, and one or two others. Perhaps we also detect a temperately expressed sense of grievance arising out of the imposition of the study of literature (to the making of which there is no end), a sense usually evincing itself in mischievous irony, as in the last two quotations. I have noticed that the possession of a quite celebrated politeness, courtesy and respectfulness does not seriously impede Eastern people in the indication of their true opinions. Very large groans can arise out of very slender little throats.

'I approve of his thought that sleep is the best time in the life. After sleep we seem fresh unless we are dozing and want to sleep again.' (In a discussion of the lyric, 'Weep you no more, sad fountains'.)

'I like to read poems as much as sleeping.'

'Milton was Puritan so he did not believe in God very much.'

'Yeats's wife went to France and saw many spirits.'

As the first two declarations show, the enjoyment of sleep is an experience too positive, the value set upon the activity too high, for this phenomenon to be described as temperate. The students were aware that nevertheless there was in educational circles a feeling (however perverse) that they ought to work as well as sleep, so these passages also bear witness to a notable honesty, a degree of courage, and no overwhelming nervousness about losing intellectual face. That is to say, hypocrisy isn't worth the effort. The student who liked to read poems as much as sleeping was thus an avid reader of poetry. In addition, we notice the realistic or earthy attitude: Thai and Singaporean students are alike in their fondness for 'coming down to earth' – and bringing literature with them. Japanese and Indians prefer to soar aloft in the vast inane. I remember an impassioned

appeal to common sense and everyday realities in an essay
by a Thai student: 'Antony and Cleopatra had many
strong emotions, but sir, it is too hot to think about them.'
(Descriptions of the sexual act – see below – are presumably
not so exhausting as descriptions of emotions.) The last
two statements demonstrate the taste for economy of argument, for the neat and cogent summing-up; they bring to
mind Ezra Pound's story in *ABC of Reading* about the
Japanese student in America who was asked the difference
between prose and poetry and replied, 'Poetry consists of
gists and piths.' And also (the lecturer is more likely to have
said that Yeats's wife went into a trance) they may be thought
to adumbrate a politely conveyed absence of wholesale
enthusiasm for foreign ways. Mrs. Yeats, France, Milton,
puritans – all true poets, alas, all of the devil's party without
knowing it – the devil of discontent!

'Shakespeare was genius in creating the quiverful quotation.'

'Festival Macbeth was a good man, but later on he became
bad.'

These are of course phonetic confusions (from the context
it was clear that Shakespeare was being praised, perhaps
this time without entire sincerity, for his equivocal passages
and rich ambiguities), but the first saying is at the least an
intelligent mishearing and pleasingly ambiguous in addition,
while the second bears witness to the Thai taste for ceremonies and anniversaries, holy days and holidays, and other
forms of 'a good time'. A man who liked festivals (especially
Buddhist ones) *would* be a good man.

'The beasts' heart was not in the sacrifice.' (Concerning the
incident in *Julius Caesar* where 'plucking the entrails of an offering forth', the augurers 'could not find a heart within the beast'.)

Here we have humour (perhaps) along with reluctance to
kill any living creature, a reluctance which causes much of
the work of slaughtering animals for food to devolve upon

the Chinese community (who, Buddhists or not, believe
that practically everything that lives is edible and may
require killing first). Our garden was rich in snakes of
different varieties, and whenever one was caught I would
call a conference of the cook, the maid, the gardener and
any neighbouring servants or passers-by who evinced interest
to decide whether or not it should be killed. These conferences were never very successful, for half the arbiters
held the snake to be absolutely harmless while the other half
maintained (with graphic miming) that if it bit you you
would fall down and expire in fearful agony. If I killed the
snake I would offend the Buddhist feelings of the first party,
if I let it go I would offend the human feelings of the second
for I should show that I didn't care what happened to them.
So I generally waited until they had dispersed and then, if it
hadn't escaped, killed the snake for the sake of the child and
her friends who were given to running round without
footwear. Perhaps I should have done better to follow the
accepted local practice, which involved lifting the snake up
on a long stick and hurling it into the next-door garden.

'Milton wrote this book (*Paradise Lost*) for telling men how
the was happened and why people must.'

'Reading poetry makes you nice and neat.'

It is very important to be nice. It is also very important to
be neat. Indeed the two are barely distinguishable. They
should be within the capacity of a properly educated person.
(The three fundamental principles of Teaching Method, so I
was told, are: the teacher should not possess any visible
physical defect, the teacher should be neatly dressed and
groomed, the teacher should not rub out the chalk on the
blackboard with his or her fingers.) As for Milton, he has
here been absolved of his puritanism, it would appear, and
is allowed some more positive attributes. The Thais display
a strong and persistent tendency to moralize, or rather to
expect other people to moralize, and they often feel unhappy

if they cannot indulge this taste. Everything must teach a lesson, preferably a moral one; the lesson does not need to be a complex one, in fact complex moral lessons are suspect (doubtfully moral, that is). That the lesson is one you have learnt before does not detract from its value: in fact this serves to set the seal of approval on the moral – there are not many morals, either, in the world – and also on the medium of the moral (that is, a poem with a good moral is a good poem). If everything is to teach us a lesson, then clearly lessons themselves, at school or at the university, must teach us a lesson. It is not difficult to deduce the lesson of *Paradise Lost* since the author has thoughtfully summarized it in the first few lines of the poem. Nor is it difficult to locate the moral of *Macbeth*: we should not kill kings. This is a moral for which the Thais have a very special devotion. The fate of Lady Macbeth serves of course to point the same moral, but if the zealous student wishes to find a secondary lesson in this case, it can well be that 'a wife should not speak to her husband in such a rude way'.

Teachers in Thai schools were worried and embarrassed when Daphne du Maurier's *Rebecca* was set as an English reader. Finally one of them went to the Ministry of Education to make representations. The conversation unfolded along these lines:

Teacher: 'The pupils ask us what *Rebecca* teaches us, and we cannot give them an answer. What *is* the answer, please?'

Official: 'The book is intended to teach them English.'

Teacher: 'But that is not enough. It is a book, and a book must convey a lesson of some sort. It must *teach*. If it doesn't teach a lesson, then they want to know why they have to read it.'

Official (sophisticated above the average): 'There are some books which we just read for pleasure.'

Teacher: 'Pleasure?'

Official: 'Yes, pleasure. We derive pleasure from reading it.'

Teacher: 'But we can't tell our pupils that! They wouldn't respect us any more!'

Rebecca came very near to being dropped from the syllabus, but happily the Ministry discovered the answer in time. *Rebecca* does teach us a lesson after all: it presents us with a picture of upper-class English life.

What is the purpose of literature? What is the use of an arts education? In their direct and simple-seeming way the Thais, as often happens, have found an answer (albeit direct and simple-seeming) to a question which other nations have evaded with elegant loquacity, erudite irrelevance and a great air of sophistication.

> 'Thai literature is full of detailed description of sexual act, which English literature is not. Or perhaps I have not read enough.'

> '. . . an allegorical comedy called "Cynthia Reveals" . . .'

> 'The rose, as the massage of unhappy lover, was sent to his girl to tell her the facts of life.' (Of the poem, 'Go, lovely rose'.)

The first writer, having boasted of his or her wide acquaintance with the indigenous literature, feels he or she had better be modest in respect of the foreign one. As regards the brief characterization of the indigenous literature, I cannot do better than quote from a paper read at a conference of South-East Asian language experts held in Bangkok in 1957: 'Great poetry is the outcome of rebellion of some kind, and the Thai has little chance to rebel, because of the satisfactory explanation of life given by Buddhist philosophy. Whatever great poetry there is in Thai is sensuous poetry, and that is one form of rebellion, rebellion against the ascetic idea of Buddhist preaching. It attempts to show that the senses are enjoyable and beautiful in contradiction to Buddhist teaching which says that the senses are painful and contemptible. The Thai language is second to none as an effective means of conveyance of such ideas.' . .

The sayings quoted above, more particularly the second and third, may indicate a knowledge (officially non-existent) of what was going on in the night-clubs, massage parlours

and little theatres down town. (Note too the interesting
anticipation of Marshal McLuhan.) Thai students manage
to give the impression of being at the same time immaculately innocent and astoundingly knowing. In one's teaching
one would proceed with the greatest caution, as if addressing
a band of particularly young and delicate nuns, only to be
greeted with a ripple of curious laughter, alerting one to
some accidental innuendo in one's discourse. One felt
like a piteously embarrassed and well-meaning bull in a
china shop, a bull who has read books about the brutishness
of bulls, and suddenly receives a sharp blow in his hind-
quarters from a flying teapot.

Women students at the university were required to wear
uniform, a simple costume of white blouse and black or
dark blue skirt, while men students were also expected to
dress neatly and soberly. Nominally this was intended to
prevent the richer girls flaunting themselves sartorially in
the face of the poorer ones, and indeed great care was taken
to avoid any sort of social discrimination in student matters.
Even so I think that the sumptuary ruling was also intended
to remind the students that they were but children. Certainly
Chulalongkorn University was one of the few educational
institutions in the world where one could be sure never to
encounter the old cliché about the purpose of education
being to teach the student to think for himself. No, education meant a preparation for Thai society as it was and, with
reasonably good luck, ever would be. If there were any
changes to be made in Thai life or society (and nothing
remains entirely static), they would be made by the appropriate authorities. And certainly not by students.

A male must never touch a female: this was part of my
prior briefing, indeed I think the whole of it. Not even a
friendly pat of encouragement on the shoulder. I was told
of an earlier cultural emissary who had disgraced himself
irrevocably by tucking a frangipani flower into some young
lady's hair: this action approximated to spiritual assault
as well as sexual, since the head is held to be the seat of the

F

soul. Quite early in my career in Thailand I found myself producing a play (by Lord Dunsany) and under the necessity of demonstrating to some of the young ladies taking part how (in accordance with the requirements of the plot) they should *pretend* to be attacking some other young ladies. (The roles were male, but we were short of male students.) They showed great interest in my instruction and intimated a wish to rehearse the incident. Therewith they fell upon me and proceeded, for all my resistance, to tear my shirt out of my trousers with signs of enjoyment, considerable strength of purpose and some success. I was rather disturbed by this, intellectually, and mentioned it to a European lady who had spent some length of time in the country. She told me, 'You mustn't lay hands on *them* – but there's nothing that says they can't lay hands on *you*.' It was obviously the case that men students were not supposed to carry away girls who had fainted, for I once saw the Dean of Arts sternly ordering some boys to put down their burden at once; they had to fetch one of the heavy stuffed armchairs which were scattered about the building, lay the unconscious girl in it, and bear both chair and body down the stairs to the nurse. Noticing my expression of concern, the Dean turned to me and shouted, 'It is only her period!'

As I suppose is to be expected, the assumption of sexlessness went along with a pervasive repression of sexuality in any of its usual and more obvious forms. The students were pure spirit, almost bodiless, certainly organless, their behaviour was studiedly demure, their bearing impeccable. Consequently the atmosphere crackled with sexual consciousness of a most exquisite kind. Yet it was not an unhappy, frustrated consciousness, it appeared to have none of the agonies ascribed to repression. It seemed to be, like sleep, positively enjoyable. In the interests of accuracy, it has to be admitted that, while the girls were content to be neat, tidy and (if possible, as it often was) very pretty, and to wait, the boys, some of them, would occasionally go to a brothel, happily and sinlessly, and generally with the knowledge of their parents. One youth, the very student who a few days earlier had rebuked me for slipping into a faintly indelicate example of sentence structure during a class, invited me to accompany him on a Sunday morning to a 'palace of pleasure', as he termed it, a place 'where humble people take their pleasure'. I shocked him again by asking if I could bring my wife too. 'You cannot take a lady, *acharn* – the ladies are *there*!'

Admirers of 'the East' commonly claim for it a wholesale spiritual superiority over 'the West', while allowing the latter a vulgar and equivocal superiority in matters technological. Where Eastern people often do have the clear advantage, I would say, is in grace. Grace of bearing, often of feature (their faces do not wear out so soon as ours), grace in everyday affairs, in their superficial relationships (so long as nothing untoward intervenes) and in their most intimate relationships. An unself-conscious dignity, an equable self-respect which is rather rare in the West – we tend to respect ourselves too much or (in an unpleasing way) too little. But grace isn't the whole of the spiritual life, and I still think that the West has shown more concern for underdogs and outcasts than has the East. It is not *only* because time lies heavy on their hands or a sense of superiority needs to be fed that you find foreign women, the wives of diplomats and businessmen, so active in organizing local charities. Nor can it be entirely accounted for as a palliation of guilt feelings. Asians are much better acquainted with the Great Chain of Being than our Elizabethan scholars are; perhaps better acquainted than our Elizabethans were. In Asian countries the person who steps outside his 'caste' (I use the word in a general sense) often has nowhere to go to but the dogs: the term 'pariah' is applied to both species. The idea of the romantic rebel, the classless or casteless hero, the 'citizen of the world', is a Western one which is gaining ground among young people in the East just as the West

is dropping it overboard. The East is predominantly conformist, not so much on principle or by 'tradition' as by
observation and rational deduction. Acceptance is not only
safer but also more decent, more graceful, than rebellion.

Western-style politics, when introduced into some Asian
countries, underwent a change: they became at the same
time all-referential and yet the property of specialists. The
man in the street or in the village was considered incapable
of political thinking, yet much of what he did or had done
to him (whatever its actual motivation) was seen as 'political'.
In Malaysia and Singapore there is an energetic and conscious
thrusting towards a more prosperous life – specially pronounced among those of Chinese race – which sometimes
looks like politics, whereas Thailand is more content to sit
on its traditional backside, to keep what it has and if possible
get more from America. This is why for the intelligent and
the industrious the former countries have more to offer at
present. In Singapore you will prosper by working; in
Thailand you will prosper, if perhaps in a smaller way, by
not doing more work (particularly in the sphere of original
thinking) than is required of you. Frustration in Thailand
is not sexual but intellectual – and perhaps this is easier to
bear. It is after all an ancient nation, unlike the others I
mentioned. And possibly the cry of the leaders of the new
countries for new talent will grow fainter in due course – for
too much talent means disgruntled intellectuals, and disgruntled intellectuals mean political trouble. Hit-or-miss
went out and 'human engineering' came in just in time for
the new countries to profit from the change.

In still other countries, what may look like politics in their
most violent form is actually the rivalry of individuals or
the power-contests of groups whose differences have little
about them that can be called 'political', if that word is
taken as implying public policies, policies conceived and
promulgated for the betterment of the human condition.
In this respect Asia leads the West, and with a degree of
panache: the whole world is moving – perhaps it has

moved – from idealism to realism, from the politics of belief to the politics of expedience. And, therefore, towards intellectual conformism, for ideas will now be of little concern or moment compared with tricks and tactics; and petty though violent squabbles will still occur within the larger framework of conformism, of intellectual lifelessness and moral lassitude. As my Thai student might well say, 'There are not much politics in the world.' This coming world, it may be, is the world of affluence, in which murder and betrayal can exist but there is no room for heroism or sacrifice. In my gloomier moments – or my more realistic ones – I fear that the realists are carrying the day – and realists, the same the world over, will accept anything which testifies to man's fallen state and distrust anything which does not.

Confessions of an English
Opium Smoker

Thus I recall, despite myself, the images
That merely were. I offer my sedate respects
To those so sober entertainments,
Suited to our day and ages.

OPIUM-SMOKING – if kept within the bounds of moderation (and the cessation of certain bodily functions which ensues upon an excess ought to be sufficient, I found, to ensure moderation), and in the case of a healthy person, that is, a reasonably well fed one, who can afford a decent quality opium, an evening's supply of which costs little more than a bottle of beer, – opium-smoking in these circumstances is not only a harmless occupation but certainly a pleasant one and even beneficial to all concerned. I have used the wrong tense. Since opium is now banned practically all over the world and is therefore available only at considerable expense and under the lowering conditions imposed by secrecy, whereby the soothing effects of smoking will be nullified by the nerve-racking vigilance, what I have written is less a testimonial than an obituary. We had to be realistic.

But to write about opium-smoking at all is incongruous, almost as incongruous as writing about the act of love. For one can hardly do so without representing it as some sort of mysterious ritual, either exotic or squalid. Nor does the current interest in and awareness of drug-taking – the pumping of filthy chemicals into the veins – help matters at all. That is a variety of masturbation, whereas opium-smoking (again with all those conditions prescribed above) has its effects, happens within, one's relations with other people and the outside world.

The atmosphere of the 'den' which we went to was more that of a rather quiet and thoughtful working-men's club. The actual smoking took a tiny amount of skill, soon acquired –

> *you pursed your lips*
> *As if to suckle and sucked your breath as if to*
> *Sigh: two skills which most of us have mastered.*

The preparation of the opium pills required more skill – but this was carried out by the 'cooks', several of whom were of Vietnamese origin and could be conversed with in a rough French. They were pleasant, gentle people, who only expected to share the pipe with you now and again, to smoke a few of your cigarettes (the opium-smoker enjoys tobacco) and to be tipped modestly. They were, presumably, addicts. I once questioned an eminent Thai doctor about the 'social problem' posed by opium-smoking – a problem on which, under the influence of the United Nations disapproval that was to cause him soon to ban opium, Marshal Sarit had begun to comment grimly during his fireside exhortations broadcast to the nation. 'Social problem?', said the doctor, 'Well, yes, opium makes the addict lazy, lackadaisical and unambitious – just like the rest of us Thais.'

Walking out of the den (it is impossible to find an un-tendentious expression in English) and into the night-life of Bangkok was like leaving a Victorian parlour to stroll in Soho. It says a lot for the civilization of the opium den, or for the benignancy of the opium, that its habitués accepted foreigners with such a friendly nonchalance. If we came to prefer our den to diplomatic cocktail parties, it was not for some excogitated reason such as that this was the 'real' Thailand. We knew it was not. The Marshal, his concubines and his large cars, his American advisers and British ad-mirers – these were real. Rural Thailand was real: those

splendid peasants, the beloved of anthropologists, with
their earthy sense of humour, and their under-staffed hospitals where at nights the patients had to take care of each
other. And most real of all were all those people, the great
majority, who went quietly about their business, smiled
at one another whenever they could and averted their
eyes when they couldn't, enjoyed whatever quality and
quantity of food they could afford, avoided political topics,
hoped the sky wouldn't fall in upon them, had probably
never seen an opium pipe in their lives, and vaguely believed
that opium-smoking was a dirty Chinese habit, possibly
displeasing to the King and unwelcome in the sight of
Buddha.

    The life of an expatriate official – it is increasingly difficult
to be an expatriate without being some sort of official of
some or other government – expatriate life in a city which
is full of United Nations agencies, diplomatic and military
missions, the seat of SEATO, ECAFE, FAO, JUSMAG,
USOM, and lots of other acronyms, and a favourite
centre for conferences and congresses, life in such a city is
peculiarly odd and confusing, because at one and the same
time you feel your activities are immensely significant and
also totally and insultingly unreal. They are significant
because they sound significant, because you are paid well for
them, and because you move in the company of other
important people doing important things. They are unreal
because if they were real, and the activities of those other
important people were real, then life would be transfigured.
And it is not. The woman squatting on the pavement outside your office and her hydrocephalic baby who is for ever
crawling a few paces to one side of her and then a few paces
to the other – they are still there. The only difference is,
the child's head is a little bigger. And you know that if you
make representations, then woman and child will be picked
up as an offence to tourists and dumped down in some other
part of the city less profitable for begging. So much for
your importance.

We liked the opium den because it was quiet, no one was seeking to impress anyone else, there were no special head-rests or special pipes for special people, the smokers had their own dignity and wouldn't beg even from rich foreigners (all foreigners were rich), no one 'represented' anything but himself or herself. Now that I look back and try to define the quiet attraction of that bleak and physically comfortless attic, it seems to me that this was almost the only setting in Bangkok where one was an equal, where one was neither a superior nor an inferior, where one didn't feel that one was living above one's social or professional or political means. To put it simply, one felt pretty well at home there. It was a good place to go to once a week or so for cleaning and repair work.

There was, however, one occasion when the English Sunday somnolence of the den was violently broken. I was not there myself, but in search of keener and more conventional and (it must be admitted) more respectable pleasures. A British businessman, a friend of a friend, was staying briefly in Bangkok, and our mutual friend had ventured that we might be ready to show him the town. We asked him if he would care to visit an opium den, and he concurred at once. But, like other visitors, once there he found the place vastly boring. It was drab, and dusty, the urinals consisted of exposed hogsheads cut down to size, there were no chairs, only bare wooden platforms to squat or lie on, no cushions but rough china head-rests, and there were definitely no pretty girls, only a sprinkling of shabbily dressed plain ones. The only beer available was the local brew, which (he said) held a headache in every sip. And he had no intention whatsoever of applying his mouth to an unhygienic bamboo tube which appeared to have been in use since the time of Commissioner Lin. As I reclined there contentedly, sipping local beer and being lackadaisically but decently massaged by a friendly fat girl, he whispered tendentiously in my ear that someone at his hotel, some American colonel, had told him about a very good show to

be seen at a little strip-theatre on Yawaraj Road. A girl
came on stage with a basket of assorted fruit, and she jiggled
round a bit, and some of her clothing fell off, and she brought
out a letter from her boy friend, and she read the letter, and
she jiggled around a bit more, and then she reached into
the basket and pulled out a banana, and . . .

Clearly the show was no place to take a lady. Nor, I felt,
was it a place to take me. But the visitor was, after all, a
visitor, and the friend of a friend. So I entrusted my wife
to the 'cooks' and drove off to find the little theatre on
Yawaraj. There are many little theatres in Bangkok's
Chinatown, but by some unlikely chance everyone of them
had switched over, apparently that very night, from strip-
tease to Chinese opera. We trudged backwards and forwards through the dust and neon, but there was nothing to
be found there except dragons and sorcerers and super-
swordsmen. Not one girl with a basket of fruit to be seen.
The visitor turned down my suggestion that we should take
a look at the opera – 'sounds like a lot of rats screeching!' –
and his dissatisfaction with his guide grew visibly. To make
matters worse, though local beer was plentiful in Chinatown, I failed to locate a bottle of the imported stuff for
him. To my further disgrace, having walked backwards
and forwards for a good hour, I had become utterly dis-
orientated and I could not find the little side-street where I
had parked the car. After more walking, and lame small-talk
contributed by me, we stumbled on the car, and back we
went to the den. It was all too clear that the visitor had
made up his mind that since in a sinful city like Bangkok
it was impossible there should not be one strip-theatre in
operation, I was for some private and doubtlessly deplorable
reason of my own depriving him of his innocent and much
looked-forward-to pleasure. Perhaps he was recalling that
well-known theory which maintains that opium-smoking
reduces sexual desire (there is another theory which holds
the precise contrary) and supposed that I had slid into utter
degeneracy and preferred pipes to bananas.

Tired and sweaty and (for his part) disgusted, we mounted to the upper storey, where my wife reclined, happy, healthy and rested. She remarked that we had missed a lot of excitement. Two men – drinkers, not smokers – had reeled into the den, downstairs, pulled out knives and stabbed each other. One died, the other was badly wounded. The police had arrived, gone through the den sternly scrutinizing its inmates, and finding no one to accuse of anything, had left.

I had succeeded in hiding from our visitor every single one of the sights of the town. He had neither smoked nor drunk; he had witnessed neither strip nor murder. We drove to his hotel in silence, we dropped him there tight-lipped, and we never heard a word from or of him again.

I remember a franker visitor to the den who, during his first and last occasion there, cried out in indignation and grief, 'Dennis, why didn't you take me to a *proper* brothel!' It was this friend who in all innocence gave us away to my boss, the British Council Representative: he couldn't believe (so he said) that so staid, so unexciting a pastime as opium-smoking could possibly be considered reprehensible.

However, respectable and cautious as British diplomatic and quasi-diplomatic officers were (and I imagine still are) in this era, careful to betray no untoward enthusiasms, but rather to show a muted and respectful attentiveness to whatever was being said or done (as no doubt befits the representatives of a power in decline), it was yet the case that while drunkenness and whoremongering were frowned on among them (as behaviour more proper perhaps to powers in their prime), the smoking of opium was a sin of another and altogether darker order. Drinking and womanizing were the foolishnesses of men, even of white men; opium was the vileness of a – of a Chinese, I suppose. It was the ultimate, the most peculiarly horrible, depravity. The next thing and one would be found propping up joss-sticks against an image of the Buddha. I often used to think of the old story about the farmer who finds his young son in the hay-loft with a milkmaid and cuffs him across the head: 'By God, next you'll be smoking!'

But I will conclude this apologia by remarking that no one who has tasted opium smoke and experienced its gently soothing operation would ever feel the slightest desire to jab a needle into his arm. I have since taken nothing stronger or more unorthodox than a couple of aspirins and, infrequently, half a Soneryl tablet when hard-pressed for sleep.

In the later part of 1958 the Government of Thailand announced that the sale and the smoking of opium would be made illegal on June 30th of the following year. The dens would remain open during the first six months of 1959 but smokers would have to register with the authorities and obtain an addict's licence. On July 1st all dens would be closed down and addicts rounded up and sent to a special hospital for treatment. The brief description of this prospective hospital given in the newspaper indicated a marked preponderance of policemen over nurses on its staff.

But already politics had intruded into the den. Juon, the young Vietnamese 'cook' whom we had known best, vanished into prison. We couldn't discover what crime he had been charged with – his friend, another 'cook' in the den, who was foolhardy enough to visit him in gaol, said that he hadn't been charged with anything. This happened at a time when lots of Communist suspects were being arrested. Marshal Sarit had recently asked the United States for increased aid, reminding them that he and his country were front-line bulwarks against Communism and currently, as could be seen, alert and active in weeding out Communists. 'People like that,' as one of Brecht's characters puts it, 'get others to do even their *weeping* for them!' And Juon, whose only political act was getting his head nearly sliced off by a Japanese sword during the war, was born to be weeded out. Mortal man, mortal man, he would fill a cell as well as better.

We are always being told that you cannot make an omelette without breaking eggs. And that living under Communism would be worse than whatever one is grumbling about. Even so, Juon wasn't an egg – and living under Communism wouldn't have been any worse for *him*. Furthermore – to argue realistically, since this is the only argument that carries weight – a country in which this sort of thing happens without audible comment is not opposed to Communism. It is only anti-Communist for as long as anti-Communism pays off. If we are obliged to buy our own freedom – by purchasing friends and then standing silently by while these friends polish off the small honest opposition we wouldn't have had to buy – then I would rather be unfree and know I was. As for Juon, he wasn't even opposition. No one who isn't an egg has much right to talk about omelettes – not in that calm, self-assured and reasonable tone of voice which suggests that you are doing eggs a favour as well as yourself.

At first the inmates of the den were cheerful enough. June 30th next year was a long way off, and laws had been passed and promulgated and rescinded in a shorter time than that. Ah Nee, the girl who would give you a drowsy massage in exchange for a few coins or a pipe or two, was saying that she would become a sempstress when the den closed, she knew of a workshop where she could get a job. A friendly 'cook' gave me a spare addict's licence of his own so that I could continue during the six months' grace. The photograph on it, though partially obliterated by an official chop, didn't look much like my face, but his intentions were good. However, I went only once during this period of grace, and the den was a desolate place. I was welcomed with more than the usual friendliness, for they were now addicts serving addicts, 'cooks' catering for 'cooks', the poor living off the poor. Ah Nee's dream of taking to needlework to earn a living had dissolved away, quite possibly the workshop had never existed except in her imagination. Poor Ah Nee, she was far too plain to take to

the streets! July 1st was now getting too near even for opium
to erase the thought of it. None of them knew what they
would do. No doubt many of them were received into that
special new hospital, for treatment by policemen and nurses.
'Before you beat the dog,' the Chinese proverb says, 'be
sure and find out the master's name': these dogs had no
master. And, as Mencius put it (and as Eastern people have
always known) 'Heaven does not speak'. But as it happened,
I was to leave Thailand before that black day came.

When the day arrived, the city's pipes were heaped up
together – it turned out that they were Government property – and publicly burnt, in one of the city's parks. Sarit
himself, I was told, attended the ceremony.

> Not the first time that fire destroys a dream.
> Coca-cola sellers slither through the crowd; bats
> Agitate among the rain-trees; flash-bulbs pop.
> A holocaust of wooden legs – a miracle constated!
> Rubbing his hands, the Marshal steps back from
> The smoke, lost in a dream of strong government . . .

Chiengmai and the Revolution

I WAS to have time only for two trips of any length
within the country. The first took me to Ubol, in the
north-east, a distressed area, short of water, but not of
cheap though sharp knives which seemed to be the chief
commodity on sale in the markets. I had gone there to visit
a set of initials called T U F E C – Thailand and United
Nations something – but I have forgotten what T U F E C
did and why I visited it.

On October 20th, 1958, I flew to Chiengmai, in northern
Thailand, on a business trip of sorts. While I was in the air
the Revolution took place. I use the officially prescribed
term for what happened when Marshal Sarit Thanarat,
with the support of the government headed by his friend
Police-General Thanom Kittikachorn, threw out the
government, proclaimed martial law, abrogated the Con-
stitution and dissolved the Assembly. This seemingly
extensive campaign was conducted smoothly and without loss of blood. There had been a number of coups
in recent Thai history, so Marshal Sarit preferred to
use this slightly misleading term for his own operation,
an operation which he explained was made necessary by
Communist subversion, or rather by certain obstacles
standing in the way of the putting down of Communist
subversion.

Chiengmai sent two soldiers to stand around at its airport,
but was otherwise unimpressed: this Revolution – or
whatever it was – was the sort of noisy, agitated and generally
incontinent behaviour to be expected of Bangkok. Since I
had arranged to give a talk the following night and martial
law now forbade congregations of more than five persons, I
had to call on the Governor of Chiengmai. The Governor,
an amiable colonel of police, said he didn't think the

prohibition was meant to apply to school children and I might as well go ahead.

It would have been better had the prohibition applied. I had expected senior school children, but the audience I found consisted mainly of small, even minute, children, already in their night attire. There was nothing to do but stumble through my lecture, on British universities, their history, administration, instructional methods, financing and so forth, abridging it severely, and then show the films I had brought with me, on Oxford and Cambridge, one of which (I have seen it several times since and it always raises a laugh in under-developed countries) is notable for its portrayal of a don in action, giving a tutorial to his pipe. At the end of the show the children had to be woken up just sufficiently to get them into bed. I discovered later that the United States Information Service had for some time been giving a regular weekly programme of old cartoon films, Mickey Mouse and Donald Duck and the like, on that night, and the children had assumed that my show was to be in the same tradition.

However, I pressed on, which was easy to do in this extremely pleasant and hospitable provincial city, full of gently moving bicycles and almost empty of cars, and during my six days there I visited seven schools (the Catholic ones struck me as the most impressive, mainly because their staff didn't behave as if they lived in a prelapsarian world), one Teachers' Training College, one Technical College, one bank, one Forest Experimental Station, one bookshop, three temples, two hospitals, one cinema, one midwifery school and three beauty queens, inquiring after their needs and discussing the ways in which the British Council might be able to help meet them. In those days Bangkok got pretty well everything that was going, and the Thai provinces almost nothing, not even (except at second hand, by telephone) a Revolution. It may well be different these days, for now there is much more going, especially in the way of sociologists, anthropologists and political scientists.

12

Downfall

BY this time I was in rather bad odour with the British Council Representative, and not too ardently loved of some senior members of the British Embassy staff. The Representative had asked me to promise on my word of honour as an Englishman not to enter an opium den again (not that he had anything against the stuff himself, but not everyone was as tolerant, for instance the Ambassador . . .), and I, as an honourable Anglo-Irishman, had felt obliged to decline to give any such word. Then there were the little poems I used to publish in the *New Statesman*, which grated on the sensibilities of the British diplomats since they felt that if Marshal Sarit should ever read them, they might grate on his sensibilities. (In retrospect I can remember only one such poem; it referred to the recent shooting of several malefactors against the wall of the National Library. It still seems fair comment: the poem respectfully opined that it was culturally deleterious to shoot people against the walls of libraries, and pointed out that in Europe we did this sort of thing more discreetly in cellars, etc.)

Then there was a lecture I gave to a hand-picked audience, more foreign than domestic, by way of 'showing the flag', which was initially an immense success, with H.E. the British Ambassador enjoying himself unconfinedly and the British Council Representative laughing himself sick. Unfortunately that was what he did do. Excess of laughter leads to excess of tears, and a week later he was feeling very sick indeed. My lecture had become 'most unfortunate'; finally it dropped a few points more and came to rest at 'deplorable'. Anyone who fancies a little research can find the lecture printed under the title, 'The Empire of the English Tongue', in *Encounter* for December 1958; a few of the darker comments were omitted from the spoken version.

Then, too, it may have been felt in a general way that politically I was (or would be if the occasion arose) a little 'soft'. And last but I dare say not least there was the fact that a high-up British diplomat considered me 'funny-looking'. (I thought he looked a bit odd too, but I didn't make an issue of it.) That the Thais, as far as I knew (though this may have been rectified later), had no objection to me was neither here nor there. As in Berlin, but now a little more markedly, I was under a cloud of indefinable wrongness. There it had been felt I would do better in the simpler-minded East; now, in Bangkok, it was being felt that I would do better in more sophisticated Europe.

This time the indefinable wrongness found definition, and quite precisely. I wantonly attacked some fifteen Thai policemen, finally obliging them to beat me up in self-defence.

This shocking behaviour occurred on an evening when I had had to decline an invitation to a party given by the Representative because of a long-standing arrangement to attend the birthday party of a close friend. Had I put duty before pleasure, no doubt the incident would still have occurred, but I imagine that the interpretation of it would have been rather different.

I would prefer not to describe the episode in detail, since I have given an accurate blow-by-blow account in a novel, *Figures of Speech*. Unfortunately I shall have to give some account, however summary, since the novel has long been remaindered. And the episode does have its exemplary interest.

Returning home from the birthday party, I found the road blocked just before our house by an empty car which had one of its doors hanging open. As we drew up to it, my wife closed the door and we drove safely past. Except that at this moment a number of what turned out to be police-men emerged from the brothel opposite under the impression that damage had been done to the car. The car was not theirs, it had been borrowed by one of them, a young lieutenant of police. Clients of the brothel were generally good-tempered, even jovial; these were not. Violence ensued with remarkable speed. As a pacifist of long standing, and indeed as an averagely sensible person (it is not only wrong but also foolish to propose physical force to a crowd of armed policemen), I offered no resistance. (Admittedly I suggested that we should send for the police, which annoyed my assailants.) My wife unwisely did offer resistance, to the extent of slapping the face of a policeman (alas, the lieutenant himself!) who was kicking my lower vertebrae in a manner reminiscent of Thai boxing, and hence I felt called upon to step between them. In fear and trembling, as I later heard, a Japanese consul was watching the proceedings from his bedroom window. But I was not Japanese. Not all the policemen were drunk, certainly, for when one of them got out his revolver, another knocked it to the ground: I was especially interested in this lesser scuffle on the fringe of the greater one.

Unhappily, though I knew some of our local law officers quite well, I knew none of these, nor did I find an acquaintance at the police station to which we were eventually taken. Here I was thrust into the communal cage (a crowded but peaceful and friendly place, rather like the opium den: one old lag pushed across a bald tyre for me to sit on, another offered a stick of mosquito-repelling incense), while my wife, since the police couldn't decide what to do with her, was thrust out into the street.

Feeling extremely sore in more ways than one, and hoping to get the problem of the brothel-parking settled once and for all, I made the gross mistake of telling my wife to ring up the British Embassy. After some lapse of time an understandably bad-tempered consul turned up at the station, and (having refused to speak to or listen to me) he concocted off his own bat some story of how I was drunk but otherwise harmless and would apologize on the morrow to the man whose face my wife had slapped. I remember signing an agreement that I would pay for the damage caused to the plaintiffs' car, for the plaintiffs were still too excited to notice that the car hadn't been touched. The money was never claimed. Through the good offices of the consul I was then transferred from the womb-like comfort of the cage to an office where two policemen bearing rifles kept watch over me through the night.

There had been painfully little evidence that night of the characteristic Thai jollity and their famous permissiveness. The guards watched with hostile suspicion from a distance – I may have been represented to them as an inveterate cop-killer – and they refused my offerings of sandwiches (brought along with coffee and cigarettes by the friend whose birth-day it had been) with an untypical brusqueness. During the tussle I had attempted to identify myself as a professor, an *acharn*, at the (I was hoping) deeply revered Chulalongkorn University or School of Great Learning. 'A professor?' they jeered, 'To us you look like a cowboy!' Cowboy, I must explain, was a slang term in current use, meaning thug or gangster. As I chain-smoked to keep off the mosquitoes' stinging, I recalled a rather similar occasion, in Egypt, in 1948, when luck had been on my side.

It was a Sunday afternoon, in Alexandria, and I was walking along the Corniche with an Irish colleague. We were on our way to take tea with the Assistant Professor of Modern History and his wife. I remarked jokingly to my friend that we were approaching an anti-aircraft gun, newly installed to protect Alexandria against Israeli attacks, and that, although no attempt had been made to camouflage it, we would be well advised not to stare as we passed. We fixed our tactful gaze in front of us, perhaps a little too fixedly, for some bystander, bored with the long Sunday afternoon, conceived the thrilling notion that we might be Jewish spies. Quickly a crowd gathered, and cries of 'Yahudi!', some questioning and some answering, broke the calm of the Corniche. Happily a small and scared-looking policeman appeared and was appropriated by the crowd before he could get away. We produced the special identity cards issued by our employer, Farouk I University, but the policeman was illiterate, and so it was decided among us that he should take us to the nearest police station as soon as possible. Standard procedure in such cases was to hail a taxi, but the policeman (possibly fearing he might be left to pay the fare) insisted hotly that the station was near, he knew a short cut, and we should therefore walk. The short cut led us through a dreadful nomad settlement – the paradox is apt – crowded with shacks made of dried mud or petrol cans, where the inhabitants were quite as bored as the loungers on the Corniche and even less well-disposed to extraneous elements. It was not a place where foreigners would normally go. Under-fed children ran between our legs looking for stones to throw. 'Yahudi?' shouted their ill-clad parents, 'Yahudi!', and our policeman quickened his pace so as to put as much distance between himself and us as was consonant with not losing us altogether. We quickened our pace in order to keep up with him, lest it should seem we were seeking to evade arrest, and also because we thought the stone-throwers might possibly be deterred by the policeman's proximity. However, these outcasts didn't seem to have much respect for policemen, and as a result of our speed we reached the police station very quickly.

Like the majority of Egyptian police stations at that time, this was a little squalid hell of its own, smelling of urine, with women squatting in the corridors weeping noisily for their arrested husbands or sons, and policemen pruriently unwinding their bandages to compare the wounds they had acquired in the course of the last student demon-strations. Here and there were gargantuan play-pens, crammed with prisoners vociferously declaring their own innocence and the guilt of others.

Relieved to be safe home again, our policeman took us into an office containing a desk, a chair and a well-fleshed lieutenant, to whom he explained the circumstances in which he had taken us into custody. The lieutenant, unimpressed by our University identity cards which (he pointed out) could have been stolen or forged, was obviously a B-feature film fan. He stared sternly into our eyes, waiting for us to break down and tell all, while we, reminding ourselves that we were only on our way to a tea party and hadn't even glanced at the guns, we tried hard to meet his gaze unflinchingly, like true British gentiles. He turned his back to us, read or pretended to be reading some document, then shot round abruptly in his swivel seat and whipped his arm out at me. 'When did you swim ashore from that Jewish ship?' he roared. I explained that I had disembarked from a British ship some eighteen months previously in Port Said, whence I had made my way overland to Alexandria with luggage and considerable difficulty. Moreover, I was a confirmed non-swimmer. My Irish friend, whose temper was not of the sweetest and whose beard seemed especially displeasing to the lieutenant, expressed a strong desire to telephone the British Consulate-General, in accordance with his legal rights. But it was a Sunday, and the British Consulate-General was closed. Now, if we were Christians, then surely we would have known it was Sunday – so reasoned the ingenious lieutenant, lost in his dream of Hollywood – and also that on Sunday such Christian establishments as the British Consulate-General were invariably closed for the day and their staff away at the seaside?

After a profound silence and a significant picking of teeth, the lieutenant arose and marched us into another room, housing his superior officer and a large group of admirers exclaiming over the latter's wisdom, his power, his wealth and probably his sexual potency too. All were drinking coffee. The lieutenant saluted his superior perfunctorily and recited the charge sheet, to the approbation and enjoyment of the coffee-drinkers. By now it seemed inevitable that we should be detained the night, perhaps in one of those over-populated play-pens, pending the reopening of the Consulate-General or the University on Monday morning. But then came the voice of one of the coffee-drinkers. 'Hallo, Mr. Enright? What are you doing here, *effendi*?' It was a clerk in the University administration whom I had met once, much earlier, when attempting to find out why my salary hadn't been paid for the previous couple of months. He vouched for me, I vouched for my colleague, and everybody smiled and exclaimed and congratulated everybody else. I suggested hesitantly that since the police had made us late for our appointment, they might like to stand us a taxi. That was the funniest joke of all. We stumbled past the prostrate women and the quarrelling policemen with laughter exploding at our heels. Drama had turned to comedy, and that was the next best thing on a boring Sunday at the police station.

But now, alas, no friendly soul was here to recognize me. And what was worse, at least one consular official had not been away at the seaside for the week-end. I began to long, slightly, for the more human atmosphere of an Egyptian lock-up, with its grand noisy emotions, its Old-Testament way of doing nothing by halves. Those wailing passage-ways, those urine-sodden walls. By the waters of Babylon. . . . Could I possibly have Jewish blood in me? I felt as if I did. But it seemed unlikely, since my father was Irish, an absent-mindedly lapsed Catholic, and my mother English (with I think a touch of Welsh), vaguely a chapel-goer, though only because she felt the Church of England belonged to Them and was socially a cut above the likes of Us. (A primitive way of dividing up the world, perhaps, but events had generally borne it out.)

I also recalled how, later in my stay in Egypt, I had been

circuitously tipped off that I was being watched by the Secret Police. So that was why I had kept coming across those outstanding personages, uncommonly noble of visage and bearing, large and healthy-looking, carrying pastoral staffs, whom I had vaguely taken for the Moslem equivalent of dandyish Roman cardinals or for Egyptian landowners who disdained to wear foreign dress. . . .? It was slightly embarrassing, because I had a number of Jewish friends, including a girl whose correspondence was being intercepted at this time. One night, as I was surreptitiously approaching the apartment house in which she lived, I was apprehended by a policeman reinforced by a soldier who searched me for concealed weapons and asked me where I was going. 'To the sea,' I said, 'The lonely sea and the sky. . . .' They shook their heads regretfully and let me go on my way.

Some months later I was called to the University administration, where it was apologetically explained to me that I had fallen under suspicion because of an entry I had made on my first arrival in the country, on a form relating to personal particulars. The registrar pushed the grimy paper across to me, indicating the sore spot with his finger. I perceived that against the question 'religion' I had declared myself a Wesleyan Methodist. Not entirely facetiously, for such had been my last religious affiliation. Wesleyan Methodism, I contended, was an eminently respectable sort of religion. 'Yes, yes,' he said sorrowfully, 'But you see, *They* thought it might be something . . . something Jewish. . . . Please Mr. Enright, if you don't mind, would you cross it out and write in something else?' 'What?' I asked, 'Church of England?' 'Oh yes,' he replied, 'that would be very good!' Feeling like an apostate I made the change, and the Secret Police at once lost all interest in me.

But no, I was not suspected of being Jewish now, that was not the point at issue. I was a cowboy.

.   .   .   .   .

It was the same old druid Time as ever. The darkness crumbled away, the bloated mosquitoes lurched off to find a shady place to sleep or procreate. My guards were replaced by fresh policemen who had missed the fun and couldn't be bothered to guard me. My birthday friend had rushed off at first light to track down the lieutenant, borrower of the car, slapper of faces and slapped of face, who was the bringer of the charge against me. Taken off guard by my distressed friend, he admitted that no damage had been done to the vehicle, and also that he and his colleagues had been drinking. He was, my friend later told me, quite alarmed to hear that I was indeed a professor. By the time the two of them reached the police station the lieutenant was ready to retract the complaint. But these just feelings were at once dissipated when he found the British consul awaiting him with arms outstretched as if to bless and the assurance of an apology from the culprit. My peace-offering was hedged about with reservations, and I was relieved to learn afterwards that, according to the consul's report, I had apologized 'with an ill grace'.

Next came our doctor (he *was* Jewish), with sad stories about the police, to attend to my black eye and slightly torn nose. I went to his surgery for an X-ray – my ribs were tender on one side – and it was established that one rib had been broken, but on the wrong side, and many years previously, probably playing rugger.

Then the real trouble started. The Representative, my chief, visited the Embassy, whence he emerged to tell me that I was a disgrace, had dragged the name of the British Council through the mud, ruined my own career with the Council (and even, it could be, damaged his, he feared) and would have to leave the country on the next plane. (I will spare the reader the other clichés; in stereotyped situations language too is apt to be stereotyped.) My own small appeal to the Embassy was fruitless: I was told that the British Council was an independent institution, that the Representative would be the first person to resent any interference by the Embassy, and that (as it happened) he was taking precisely the same action as would be taken by them in similar circumstances involving one of their staff. This didn't check too well with the Representative's defensive remark, when friends interceded for me, that the British Embassy didn't like having writers about the place. (Poets and novelists, presumably, for they would hardly object to literary critics.) But then, when men band together to accomplish a good end, we cannot expect the means they use to be wholly immaculate.

Thoughtful readers, zealous for fair treatment, may argue that trained and expensive diplomats have better things to do than rescue their weaker compatriots from the local police. While I see the force of this proposition, I cannot say that I noticed the British Embassy in Thailand doing or saying very much apart from agreeing totally with whatever the American Embassy was doing or saying. Even so, it was my fault, and I shouldn't seek to evade responsibility. My Thai friends pointed out at once how foolish it was of me not to ring them; one of my closest colleagues was married to a senior prince who would soon have turned the tables, or at least steadied them. However docile the Thais may seem to be, however conformist, they are not so simple as to assume that justice inevitably prevails or that people who get into trouble with the police are invariably of a criminal disposition. Thus they responded, 'Oh yes . . . our policemen!', while the British Head of Chancery told me that the behaviour I attributed to the Thai police on the night in question was 'entirely out of character'.

It was this remark, together with two other incidents, which led me to surmise that the limits set upon the exercise of their intelligence could have the effect of causing our undoubtedly intelligent diplomats to behave at times in a manner quite staggeringly stupid. The first incident occurred in Japan, when an emissary from the British Embassy in

Tokyo proposed that from time to time I should report to them on the incidence of Leftist views among my Japanese colleagues. I was well placed for this, he told me, since I had no overt connection with the British establishment. When I pointed out that for all he knew I might be a bit Leftist myself, in which case my reports would be less than wholly reliable, he replied, 'No need to worry there – the necessary adjustments would be made.' The low esteem in which I was held (quite rightly) as a source of information was to be deduced from the reimbursement offered: an occasional free trip to Tokyo. The second disillusioning incident occurred in the course of my present story. The clinching argument in favour of my leaving Bangkok forthwith – clinching because of its appeal to self-interest – was (the Head of Chancery informed me) that my name was now down in city police records and therefore, should the Communists take over the country, the British Embassy would be unable to save me from their wrath. True, I had observed plainly enough the Embassy's inability to save me from the wrath of a few drunken cops. . . . Yet, not being an anti-Communist myself but merely opposed to Communism, it flashed through my mind that if the Communists did sweep through Thailand, then we should *all* be in bad trouble – with the possible exception of myself, a registered victim of the corrupt American-subsidized police of the ancient régime. The diplomat's argument serves as a nice illustration of one of the minor uses of Communism in our time.

This whole episode taught me a useful lesson, something which I had been in danger of forgetting as I called at the Embassy commissary to collect my tax-free liquor and smokes – if you live abroad, then live abroad, and don't slip into the bad habit of remembering you are an Englishman on those occasions when you think it will work to your advantage. I had sent my nasty little poems to England by the diplomatic bag – and now justice both diplomatic and poetic had been rendered me. Writers, above all, ought to know that where they are concerned there is no such thing as diplomatic privilege.

The novel which I thereafter wrote turned out rather a flop, sad to say. The chief reason for writing it was that I wanted to get the record reasonably straight. The accounts I had heard from various quarters, mostly from people passing through Singapore on their way from Bangkok, departed considerably from the facts. Almost all these variants had one common factor: my wife did not appear in the story at all. And the favourite version, besides leaving her out, changed the venue of the fracas from the street outside the brothel to a staircase inside it. In part it was the wish to tell the truth that accounted for the novel's weakness: another instance of the naïve failure to understand that a literary work is an artefact, a thing in itself, and not a means to inform or correct. In addition I had worked so hard to get the tone right, to expunge self-commiseration or self-congratulation, that I had left the writing without any tone at all. Apart from some of the provincial papers, who are readier to accept studies in 'local colour', reviewers mostly found the story boringly improbable, even incredible. The *Daily Telegraph* remarked sadly that while the author couldn't possibly believe the Far East to be characterized by bumbling Westerners, he certainly wrote as if he did. Ah me, I suppose the version which has me lustfully rampaging inside the brothel is more convincing, after all!

13

The Home Front

WE packed our belongings, sold what belongings we couldn't pack, found a home for the servants and our Siamese cat, and were in London in no time. Homeless and jobless – but not salary-less, for by a happy chance I had signed up with the British Council for another year in Bangkok shortly before the battle of the brothel. It was April 1959, and the weather was marvellous, which was a great help, for at first we had only a room in an hotel near Gloucester Road station. London was at its best (the natives of course grumbled about the heat), and this was just as well, because I have an incontinent sort of imagination which tends to forget who owns it and shows me myself as others see me or in an even worse light. London in sunlight was reassuring, and so were the British Council headquarters in Davies Street.

My boss had offered me a deal whereby if I agreed to leave Thailand quietly, ostensibly on leave (for which I was then due), he would agree to make no reference to opium-smoking and other minor lapses in his report to Head-quarters. His concern was to obviate scandal which would mar the good reputation of the British Council, if not of Britain, in Thailand. My own feeling was that to sneak away, leaving the University under the impression that I would be coming back after the vacation to carry on my work, would be at least equally damaging to various reputations – including my own. Also, I had not the slightest intention of leaving without saying good-bye to friends. Also, I fear, I desired the selfish satisfaction of a fight, since I have always believed that if you kick a man, then he has the inalienable right to cry out. And I suspect that I even had some tiny hope of reversing the situation.

So Headquarters received the complaint against me in full
(they received so many complaints from all over!) and I
presented my case to a group of benign senior officials
verbally. Their kindliness undid me. Before long it appeared
that I had been the innocent victim of jealousy, of high-
handed and (strictly speaking) officially improper behaviour. . . . It is naturally disconcerting to find oneself considered more innocent than one believes oneself to be: this
is the soft answer that does turn away wrath. I was assured
that the Representative had exceeded his brief and would be
duly reprimanded, and that, though unfortunately there
was no suitable alternative overseas posting available at
present, I should continue to receive my salary. In return
perhaps I would be good enough to do various little jobs
for the Council from time to time (indeed I would! I
didn't want charity), such as helping to sieve through the
many applications which the Council received for posts in
the Far East, that part of the globe on which by now I
was such an authority (oh yes, I would be very glad to
sieve applications!).

Many of these applications, I was told (and have since, as
head of a university department, confirmed), were of a
totally unsuitable kind, being really applications for pro-
fessions and duties and activities which were not being
advertised. The applicant wanted to go to Thailand, not to
teach English, but because he was thinking of becoming a
Buddhist; or he was keen to get to Japan, not to teach literature, but because he had gathered that the penalties against
homosexuality were considerably lighter there; or as a
sceptical Thai lady, lately my colleague, had put it, he just
wanted to escape from the English climate or from mother.
I was very ready to assist the British Council in the selection
of suitable persons, and from time to time I would ring
them to ask when my services were required. From time to
time they would get in first and ring me to say that perhaps
next week or in a fortnight's time they might be calling
upon my services.

I was never called upon. Every now and then I would visit my employers; I discovered a back door to the premises, which enabled one to gain access to the offices without the remarkably efficient receptionist at the front intervening to prevent or give the alarm. How well I remember the sad, patient look on the faces of those various desk-bound home officers, in Personnel or Far East office or Teaching-of-English-Overseas, when they saw the Ancient Mariner, the scarred old soldier prematurely retired from 'the field', peering ominously through their door. Before very long the back entrance was locked on the inside. And so mostly I stayed at home – we had been lucky enough to find a furnished flat in St. Martin's Lane – reading and reviewing current fiction for the *Spectator*.

The only little job I did for the Council at this time was to draw up a first list of fifty British books suitable for printing in cheap editions and dissemination in foreign lands. My list began with *Treasure Island* and ended with a more or less popular book on the economics of everyday life, and the compiling of it helped to keep me occupied for quite a while since I found that I had to read or re-read each book rather carefully and in a special frame of mind. I included a good children's book by the Victorian writer, E. Nesbit, *The Story of the Treasure Seekers*, but had to append a note recommending the elision of the ejaculation 'nigger' on p. 184; similarly the *Memoirs of Sherlock Holmes* struck me as an excellent choice for an early entry in the list, until I noticed that one of the stories was called 'The Yellow Face'. This may seem over-nervousness, but we were unable to teach any Conrad at all in Thailand because of the rude remarks passed on the Thai flag and its 'Noah's Ark elephant' by the chief mate in *Typhoon*. Whether my list ever served any purpose other than keeping me quiet I don't know, but the Council were kind enough to pay me a fee of £30 for it.

. . . . . .

It had been arranged much earlier that during my leave I should undertake a fortnight's lecture tour in Germany for the Cultural Relations section of the Foreign Office, and despite the large disgrace I had since fallen into, no one thought it necessary to cancel this plan. I spent about half of the fortnight in West Berlin and, as I have mentioned, was then offered a post at the Free University. One reason why I declined was that I had resolved to get back into that part of the world from which I had been ejected. Prince Prem Purachatra, the head of the Department of Modern Languages at Chulalongkorn University, had promptly and gallantly sent a protest against my withdrawal, and I had been invited back to the University to join its staff, but . . . I felt I had better find somewhere else in the East. It was not the vengeance of the police I was afraid of so much as the diplomats.

One day my presence was asked for in Davies Street to meet the Director-General of the British Council. Was I to get an apology, a medal, a desirable posting? I didn't really think so. The Director-General, a hard-headed and masterful man who had served in the Treasury and as First Civil Service Commissioner before assuming his present position, was popularly supposed to be engaged in making the British Council respectable in the eyes of Whitehall and the Treasury. He told me he had gathered that I had written a book – this was a novel which I haven't mentioned hitherto, called *Insufficient Poppy*, at that time in the press – a book which was the sort of book that the British Council could not have their officers writing, not even contract employees like myself. He had not himself read the book, nor did he intend to. He understood that the Council had suggested that I should withdraw the book from publication or myself from the Council, and I had declined the first alternative. The Council had been fortunate to have my services in the past – but I would understand that it would not be able to avail itself of them in the future. He hoped nevertheless that it would not be necessary to cut the painter altogether.

The significance of this curious metaphor emerged when he went on to say that he had heard I might be going back to Japan – in fact Waseda University in Tokyo had put out vague feelers – and if this were so, then the British Council would be prepared to pay the fares for me and my family, one way. Though at the time I felt mildly resentful of his tone in referring to my poor book – it had many defects but at least it was remote from the pornographic – I was glad to have received such a clear and unambiguous statement of policy on the question of publications: the painter had been well and truly cut, and not just one way. The gentler or more sentimental officials with whom I had dealt hitherto, weak-mindedly reconciled to the thought that it was in the nature of writers to write, had found no better formula than to rely on my discretion. Clearly I was weak in this quality, and (I suspected) not likely to grow stronger hereafter.

To wind up this story, I must add that the British Council – not the Director-General but some other department of it – invited me to participate in a forthcoming lecture tour of India, a two-months' intellectual Odyssey beginning in December of that year, along with two British professors, William Walsh, of Leeds University, and Peter Butter, then of the Queen's University of Belfast. It was a strange place, that building in Davies Street, and perhaps it still is. A blessing on its head! Cringing one's way out of one office, a broken man, an exposed pornographer, whoremonger, dipsomaniac and opium addict, one's painter torn to ribbons, one would enter another office to find oneself a hero of labour, an expert, a distinguished academic, besought on almost bended knees to be gracious enough to fly first class to India and spread one's sweetness and light. . . .

I do not speak in scorn. Perhaps the British Council, at least at Headquarters, represented the British way of life more accurately than they may have supposed. I was recompensed for the ill-treatment and embarrassment I

H

had received by being offered two months in India, while my erstwhile chief, the Representative in Bangkok, was recompensed for the ill-treatment and embarrassment he had suffered by being awarded, shortly afterwards, the Order of the British Empire. 'Ambiguous gifts,' in both cases, 'as what gods give must be,' and yet undoubtedly of a lenitive effect.

It was altogether a silly affair, and its ending, when once the tragic possibilities had melted away, was entirely appropriate. All the same, looking back on it I am disquietened to think how it could have worked out for someone less able to defend himself, someone more dependent on official good will or immaculacy of reputation. And indeed, how much nastier it could have been for me were the British Council and the Foreign Office more monolithic than apparently they are.

14

A Small Moral Victory

TWO years before, while in Berlin, I had put in for the
Chair of English at the University of Malaya in Singapore (now the University of Singapore). Finally the University authorities had got round to offering me the post, but
by then I had already signed on with the British Council
to go to Bangkok. Very conveniently – for such opportune-
ness is rare in the experience of a mendicant – it turned out
that the man who had taken the post in Singapore was now
relinquishing it after only two years of tenure. I applied
again, for this seemed my chance to re-infiltrate the East.
On this occasion, since I was in London, the Inter-University
Council for Higher Education Overseas, acting as Singapore's intermediary, summoned me for interview. I wasn't
too gratified by this, remembering my previous appearance
in their cellar, for it seemed to me that having offered me
the job before, they should feel no need for an interview
now. Though, of course, I was now two years and one
country older in experience. I wondered what the benign
old gentleman would have to say this time – fighting with
policemen was certainly something a university wouldn't
want!

However, he was not a member of this board of selection.
Instead there were two extremely distinguished 'home
university' professors of English, both of them literary
critics. Little of academic import passed across the table,
except that when asked what changes I would make in the
department if appointed, I lamely suggested that I might
cut down on the eighteenth century. I had visited the
University of Singapore, from Bangkok, as external
examiner for the English finals the previous year, and it
had struck me that the Graveyard Poets loomed larger than
was needful. Unhappily one of the professors, a specialist in

the eighteenth century, thought I was intending to rip Dr. Johnson out of the syllabus. But mostly I was occupied in attempting to explain how it was that I had held so many posts so briefly in so many different countries. The other professor had uttered the rather hard word, 'butterfly': it was not the first time I had been compared with this unsatisfactory form of life. But what could I do? Should I lead the gentlemen through the sequence of events and accidents, understandings and misunderstandings, first in Berlin and then in Bangkok? No, that I felt would be the end of my candidature: there were worse things than butterflies.

The second professor, a famously austere and scrupulous man, went on to say that what they wanted was someone who would settle down and make a good job of reorganizing the department. The department had seemed reasonably efficient to me – and if it had been totally deficient then I certainly wouldn't be able to fling unwanted members of staff out on their ears – but I asked how long he would expect the person appointed to stay in Singapore. 'Oh, about seven years,' he replied. A magic number. As I say, I had spent a little time there and I had friends on the staff, and I knew something of the difficulties which the University faced as a colonial foundation in a newly independent country. To get into the country in the first case I should need a work permit – and work permits were issued by the new Singapore Government, not by the Inter-University Council. And so I tried to point out that the length of my stay might not be determined solely by my own wishes, but the attempt was not very successful. I was reminded of the time I set out to explain to the sweet old rector of Chulalongkorn University – a truly saintlike man, he was later sacked by Marshal Sarit for failing to foresee and preclude a minor student demonstration – that I was about to leave the country because I had fallen foul of some uncouth policemen outside a brothel. I had given up after the first few words.

I was reminded too of how I had been asked to promise never again to enter an opium den. Now I was being asked to furnish an assurance that, if appointed to Singapore, I would stay put for seven years or so. I felt like a guilty schoolboy whose prefabricated excuses falter on his trembling lips as he feels the cool, incorruptible gaze of the headmaster upon him. Having too much to say can leave one as speechless as having too little. And much more vexed.

Nothing further happened for a long time, but eventually and somewhat to my surprise I was offered the post. I was in Delhi at the time, on the first leg of the British Council lecture tour. My family had stayed in London, not knowing where they would be going next, the bulk of our belongings once again lying in bond. I cabled my wife to make reservations on a ship reaching Singapore at about the time I would get there at the close of the tour.

There was a rather amusing sequel to this board of selection. My later dealings with the Inter-University Council have been considerably pleasanter, for this body has been of great help in recruiting staff for Singapore, and I have been on the other side of the table. When in London on leave a few years ago, I went along to their office to arrange to interview candidates for posts in English and asked to see the file containing the applications. A clerk was sent to locate this file, and she returned bearing several large folders which she dumped into my lap. As soon as I opened the top one I realized that it contained the entire past history of the staffing of the English Department; I also realized that I had opened it at the confidential report on the interview which I had attended in 1959. Amused by this quaint accident, I began to read. But before long, although I was quite alone in the room, I found myself getting horribly embarrassed, I was even blushing. I stopped at the point at which the report was pointing out quite correctly that though the candidate was not a scholar in the accepted sense of the word, he had nevertheless had an extensive experience of the East, and I closed the folder fearfully and placed it on a chair at some distance from the one I was sitting on.

I had also noticed in those brief moments that there was only one other candidate short-listed, and he appeared to be neither a scholar nor particularly experienced in anything whatsoever, so it was not so surprising after all that I had been offered the post.

As I write this I have completed seven and a half years in Singapore, *in situ*. It has been touch and go at times – more than once the suitcases have been hauled out of the cubby-hole under the staircase and dusted down – and there is no guarantee that the butterfly will be resting on the same leaf when this book is published. Even so, and I say this with petty-minded pride, I have for what it is worth, by dint of silence, exile, cunning, hysterics, sloth, 'low posture' (as the sociologists call it) and simple-mindedness, exceeded the period desiderated by the professor. A sort of victory.

15

Singapore

A ND so we came to Singapore. It was a part of the
world, one felt at first, where the East had been sadly
diluted with the West, the Orient's native hues sicklied o'er
with the pale whitewash of British hegemony. But as time
passed I found, my own curiosity diluted perhaps, that I
was even preferring a diluted Orient. Customs and traditions are not inevitably ways of enriching life or personality,
quite often they are ways of limiting or impoverishing – a
geisha is not a woman plus, but a woman minus – which
thus, one must admit, makes them of particular value in
poor or over-populated countries. Singapore had no traditions in this sense, or only a number of diverse, imported
and rather faded traditions. Singapore had nothing to fall
back on but its humanity, and (it seemed to me, rightly or
wrongly) it could afford to fall back on that. At least there
wouldn't be too much of that initially fascinating but finally
stifling reference to tradition and national character. Better
a country with all before it than one with too much dragging
at its heels.

At this time the students all came from English-medium
schools, they had taken the Cambridge Overseas School and
Higher School certificates, and though they didn't invariably
feel that Japanese fascination of what's difficult, they were
certainly much more proficient in English. The department's standards appeared to be creditably high. Student
numbers were small, relatively to Japan extremely small, no
one seemed strikingly penurious, suicides were minimal,
nervous breakdowns were more a sign of affluent sophistication than of desperate spiritual stress, and there was much less
coyness than among the Thais. This too came to have its
selfish attraction for me, since I had reached a stage at which
the most likely nervous breakdown seemed my own.

Based on the British model, the University was governed in its various spheres by sub-committees, committees, boards, Faculties, Senate, Council and Court, and this administrative hierarchy, if wasteful of time, seemed likely to ensure that academic earnestness and moral justice should generally prevail, and a reasonable degree of autonomy be preserved. It was true that the People's Action Party, still in its first year as the first independent Government of Singapore, was not too well disposed towards the University. This was a colonial foundation, inevitably, and the People's Action Party (hereafter referred to by its initials, P.A.P.) was of the opinion that the University, more specifically the students, had played no very noble part in the ousting of the British. The students were knowingly the *élite*, trained in the language of the colonial power, with safe jobs in the middle reaches of the Civil Service to look forward to – and therefore politically apathetic. But judging by historical processes as they had unfolded elsewhere, it seemed probable that the students from the Chinese-medium schools and the Chinese-medium university, Nanyang, who had been active against the British, would now continue active against the P.A.P., and therefore the Government would come to form a more appreciative view of the apathy of the English-educated. In any case the Government needed English-educated graduates, for it didn't appear likely that the administration of the country could be carried on in Chinese, not under the P.A.P.

The Malay language, in practice a low-level lingua franca of the area, was made much of by the politicians, but mainly as a linguistic red herring to distract attention from the real problem, or the real problem as reflected in the rivalry between the English and the Chinese languages. English was the (theoretically) polluted tongue of the colonialist power; Chinese was the language of Peking. Chinese had immense emotive power, of a sort which could be useful but also dangerous and was difficult to control, while English in a wider setting possessed the negative charm of political neutrality and of course a large commercial utility. It had taken root as the language of administration and the courts, and it was the language in which nearly all of the P.A.P. leaders had been educated and in which they were ideologically most articulate. It was not – a fact which cut both ways – the language of the Communists who in their crude, dedicated manner had done most to speed the British on their way. Malay was the tongue of the peasants, of those who considered themselves the true indigenes and original possessors of the land, and in Singapore it was the language of the gardeners and syces – and thus it suited well as the nominal 'national language' for as long as it took the P.A.P. to establish themselves firmly and find out what their post-independence political line was to be.

Thus there existed a balance of power, linguistically speaking, and however nervous the balance and whatever ups and downs the future might bring, it was clear that English was here to stay. One could therefore, it seemed, expect to pursue a respectably academic life, reasonably peaceful but not excessively placid, and maybe even for as long as the seven years stipulated by the board of selection in London.

Since there was a queue of new professors I didn't get round to delivering my so-called inaugural lecture until November. In the meantime I had come to like and respect our students. That they were in some degree 'anglicized' seemed to me no bad thing; and it certainly made it easier to teach them English literature. I have never had any objection to anglicization: it is the *pure* English who worry me – a race that stews in its own juice is bound to turn rancid in the course of time.

Singapore, I had better explain, was at this time undergoing a sort of cultural spring-cleaning. A new Government, especially when it is the first national Government, must naturally busy itself, like any other new broom, and when

the lot of the people under colonial rule has not been a notably harsh one, it will be correspondingly difficult to find
something to be visibly busy about. The Chinese seem
somewhat sceptical as regards such concepts as liberty and
independence and self-determination. This is not because
they lack pride, but rather because they have so many other
and more concrete things to be proud about. And in the case
of Singapore, most of the inhabitants were immigrants or
the children of immigrants, and perhaps they had failed to
notice that the island was a colony, or else perhaps they saw
themselves as colonists rather than as oppressed natives. (A
view of the Chinese sometimes held by the Malays, who
would see themselves in the role of the oppressed natives!)
After all, they had come to Singapore, or their forefathers
had, because life in Singapore and Malaya was easier, perhaps freer, than life in China or India.

From its inception, or perhaps one should rather say from
its assumption of power, right up to the present, the P.A.P.
has always had more energy than outlet, more drive than
elbow-room. This is a situation apt to generate irritability
in a party's leadership and a tendency towards the dis-
proportionate taking of umbrage. It may account for why,
though P.A.P. leaders have repeatedly described the local
populace as 'sophisticated', nevertheless they have often
treated them like naughty or backward children. In the
earlier days of its régime, the P.A.P. was distinctly school-
mistressy, in a petty, bullying fashion. One way of being a
new brush, of evincing themselves as the brave new successors to the insufficiently hated British, was to launch a
campaign against 'yellow culture'. 'Yellow culture' soon
grew into a large, pervasive, inclusive and ill-defined concept, which ranged from juke-boxes to Wordsworth's
daffodils, from prostitution (another colonialist importa-
tion) to films with a racialist tendency, and somewhere near
its centre came strip-tease, the Leftist-cum-lascivious fictions
of Han Suyin and, for a time, myself.

The object of the campaign was to sweep out 'yellow

culture', all of course directly or indirectly of foreign origin, in order to make way for a 'local culture' which was even less defined than the yellow variety, or defined only in terms of the ousting of the latter. If you cry out loud and long enough against a set of objects or practices, you will for a time give the impression of actually offering and promoting another set. This desiderated culture, to be manufactured under the invigilation of the Government, was to be immaculately hygienic, moralistic, socialized, inoffensive to Malays, to Chinese, to Indians, to Ceylonese, to Eurasians, to Moslems, to Buddhists, to Christians (whether Catholics, Methodists or Seventh Day Adventists), to Hindus, to Sikhs, to atheists, to vegetarians and carnivores, and to all shades of colour from the whiter-than-white Chinese to the blue-black Tamil. It was fairly obvious that no work of art, at least no composition containing words, could cope with all these prescriptions or proscriptions. It needed no great intellectual or intuitive powers on my part to perceive, after a few months in the country, that the exhortations and admonitions of the Ministry of Culture, far from encouraging the 'right kind' of local writing, were simply discouraging writing of any kind. Not only was there no money in it and precious little glory, as would-be writers had discovered in British times, but now there was a definite risk attached! For somebody, somewhere, somehow, was bound to be offended, or (since he had been by implication encouraged to do so) to claim to be offended. There is nothing that so conduces to the proliferation of susceptibilities as telling people how susceptible they are.

And, in the nature of things, no one was more susceptible to offence on the score of culture than the Minister of Culture himself.

16

Yellow Professor

Politics in a work of literature are like a pistol-shot
in the middle of a concert, something loud and vulgar,
to which it is not possible to refuse one's attention.

STENDHAL

MY inaugural lecture, delivered on November 17th 1960, was a great success, at the time. So, I should have remembered, was the one I gave in Bangkok on the Empire of the English Tongue. In the heat of the moment the Acting Principal, a medical man, introduced me as Professor Ensign, adding to the jollity of the occasion and also (as was to be seen later) striking an aptly warlike note at the outset of an action which in certain quarters was interpreted as an aggressive one. My subject was 'Robert Graves and the Decline of Modernism', but since this was an inaugural lecture I began with a few topical remarks on culture, its equivocal nature and the acquisition or creation of it – commonplaces, admittedly, but only the aesthete and the university poet despise commonplaces.

The next morning I awoke, fully inaugurated, to find that the local English-language paper, the *Straits Times,* had printed a report of the proceedings under banner headlines, ' "HANDS OFF" CHALLENGE TO "CULTURE VULTURES",' followed by what I can only assure readers that even then I recognized as a provocative sub-heading: 'University professor talks of juke-boxes and pantuns . . . and says "let the people make their own choice".' The report was tendentious (as Bernard Levin pointed out in a neat retrospective survey of the Affair printed in the *Spectator,* no mention was made of the subject of the lecture and the name of Robert Graves appeared nowhere in it), but at least it got its snippets right, for I had passed a copy of the complete lecture to a reporter who was too lazy or busy to attend it:

'A British poet, author and critic, Professor D. J. Enright to-night fired another salvo at Government-sponsored attempts to create culture, and stressed that the most important thing for the two Malayan territories to do at present was to remain "culturally open".

He said that authority must leave the people to fight their own battles, especially their personal battles. And he maintained that culture "is something personal".

Mr. Enright also deplored the Singapore Government's ban on juke-boxes, spoke of the futility of instituting a "sarong culture complete with pantun competitions", and suggested that every culture contained a trace of "yellow".

He made these points while giving his inaugural lecture at the University.

He first attacked the Singapore Government's attempts to create a Malayan culture and destroy "yellow culture" in an article in the latest issue of the *Malayan Undergrad*, the mouthpiece of the University Students' Union.

In his speech tonight, Professor Enright held that culture was built up by "people listening to music and composing it, reading books and writing them, looking at pictures and painting them, and observing life and living it".

Using the word "culture" in its widest sense, he said, the cultures of the Old World could be described as "extremely cultural in the sense of being very distinctive, idiosyncratic, very different one from another".

He added: "Today the most distinctive national cultures are those which involve cannibalism, head-shrinking, or other forms of human sacrifice."

"These days 'national culture' is chiefly something for the tourists from abroad – the real life of the country goes on somewhere else."

Professor Enright said that to institute "a sarong culture, complete with pantun competitions and so forth" at this point would be as ridiculous as "to bring back the maypole and the morris dancers in England just because the present monarch happens to be called Elizabeth".

He added: "The important thing for Singapore and Malaya is to remain culturally open."

"Who can decide in advance which seeds will fall on barren ground and which will grow?"

Claiming that all culture contained a trace of "yellow", Mr. Enright said: "Art does not begin in a test-tube, it does not take its origin in good sentiments and clean-shaven upstanding young thoughts."

It begins, he said, "where all the ladders start, in the foul rag-and-bone shop of the heart."

To obtain art, and build culture, he suggested the following method: "Leave the people free to make their own mistakes, to suffer and to discover."

"Authority must leave us to fight even that deadly battle over whether or not to enter a place of entertainment wherein lurks a juke-box, and whether or not to slip a coin into the machine."

Professor Enright warned that "a totalitarian state affords the most civilized society one can have," because "temporarily, at any rate, its citizens are essentially dead."'

Even so, when later in the morning a call came from the Ministry for Labour and Law requesting me to report there that afternoon 'on a matter concerning your passport', I wondered whether it mightn't be a hoax on the part of a Philosophy teacher who was notorious for his sense of humour. (He had once rung a colleague of mine, in disguised accents, in the middle of the night, purporting to be a man whose wife was that moment engaged in unexpected and difficult childbirth, and imploring 'the doctor' to come at once. When my colleague protested that he was no doctor, or no medical doctor, but only a doctor of philosophy, he was roundly reviled for misleading the public by describing himself as doctor in the telephone directory . . .) However, the departmental secretary rang the Ministry clerk back and established that the call was genuine. The clerk could not or would not explain what was afoot.

The treatment which had been prepared for me was on the lines of that traditionally meted out by the stern White master to the offending native. Having been kept waiting for some time on a glum wooden bench outside, I was called into an office and berated loudly and fiercely in a language which I couldn't understand. The Acting Minister for Labour and Law, ostensibly in charge of proceedings because I was being threatened with the loss of my work permit but actually given this leading role because he was the one Malay minister at the time, uttered some rude and wounding remarks in Malay, and these were then kindly translated into English for my benefit by the Minister of Culture, a Ceylonese by origin. It was, in fact, a case of the translation preceding the original; and almost as ingenious a touch as summoning some wog to the Home Office and upbraiding him in Welsh.

I had furnished myself with my passport and a copy of the lecture *in extenso*, but the Acting Minister for Law (the Minister himself was currently in Japan, incidentally, where rumour had it he was studying Japanese techniques for the abolition of prostitution) didn't want the passport and the Minister of Culture wouldn't have anything to do with the lecture. 'Did you or did you not say this?' he demanded, waving a copy of the day's *Straits Times*. I sought to explain that while I had indeed said that, I had said a good deal more, and that the reporting of the *Straits Times* was so selective (not to say sensational) as to be in effect tendentious. I asked the Minister to read the whole lecture as delivered but, rather like the Director-General of the British Council on an earlier occasion, he shuddered with distaste at the prospect. He thrust a document upon me, telling me that if I once more interfered in local politics I should be deported forthwith, and concluded the interview by saying, 'We are running things now – not you!' An odd remark, that last bit, I thought.

Of course the Minister didn't wish to read my lecture, and of course no conceivable explanation would have served me at this stage, for the document which he handed me had already gone out as a Press release. This was a point which was later to be conveniently forgotten by all concerned, including myself.

The document took the form of a letter and ran as follows:

'Dear Sir,

In January this year you were granted a professional visit pass to take up appointment as professor of English at the University of Malaya. Your duties were to supervise the teaching of English at the University.

Since then, it would appear, you have arrogated to yourself functions and duties which are reserved only for citizens of this country and not visitors, including mendicant professors.*

On two occasions you have used the facilities afforded you as professor of English to involve yourself in political affairs which are the concern of local people.† The Government has made clear before and after the elections that it will not tolerate any alien like you who misuses our hospitality by entering the political arena.

Whether the Government is right or wrong in banning juke-boxes or whether it should or should not try to foster a Malayan culture is a matter for the citizens of this country to decide. We have no time for asinine sneers by passing aliens about the futility of "sarong culture complete with pantun competitions" particularly when it comes from beatnik professors.

* It is interesting to note that when the Italian Jesuit missionary, Father Matteo Ricci, turned up in China in 1601, he was described in an official document as 'a mendicant . . . where he comes from it is impossible to say, the alleged name of his country being untraceable in our records.' (See Dennis Bloodworth, *Chinese Looking Glass*, London, 1967.)

† The first occasion was the passing of a few remarks on the nature of culture to a student reporter who wrote them up as a paragraph for the *Malayan Undergrad*. While I can understand that this would not have escaped the jealous vigilance of the Ministry of Culture, I am astonished that the *Straits Times* should have taken note of such a trivial item.

This is to inform you that should you again wander from the bounds of your work for which you were granted entry into the country, then your professional visit pass will be cancelled as in all such cases. You are being paid handsomely to do the job which you are presumably qualified to do, and not to enter into the field of local politics which you are unqualified to participate in. You would do well to leave such matters to local citizens. It is their business to solve these problems as they think fit. They have to live and die in this country. You will be packing your bags and seeking green pastures elsewhere if your gratuitous advice on these matters should land us in a mess.*

The days are gone when birds of passage from Europe or elsewhere used to make it a habit of participating from their superman heights of European civilization.

If you bear this in mind your stay in this country may be mutually profitable.'

The letter was signed 'Ahmad bin Ibrahim, Ag. Minister for Labour and Law.' A sick man at the time, Inche Ahma died not very long afterwards.

Dutifully the Press and radio disseminated the text of what they permitted themselves to call 'an unprecedented rebuke'. With a heavy heart my wife faced the prospect of packing the suitcases only so recently unpacked. 'It's not so bad for you,' she said, as she had said in Bangkok and on other distressful occasions, 'You can write about it, it's all material for you. But we . . .' And indeed as Cavafy – to-

---

* This argument was to come up again and again during the following years. When an expatriate teacher indicated dissent from Government policy he was told that he had no stake in the country and therefore *he* wouldn't have to abide the evil consequences of his advice or criticism, he would have somewhere to run away to. The Prime Minister recently declared in a meeting at the University that he was only prepared to trust people who had to stay in Singapore and face the music simply because they had nowhere else to go to. The argument against expatriate intervention would be more cogent were it not that local citizens have been loth to disagree with the Government precisely *because* they do not have anywhere to go to, except prison.

I

gether with Brecht, a poet whom I have found especially
congenial, especially apropos – has written:

> To you I have recourse, O Art of Poetry,
> You in a way know something about drugs;
> Attempts to numb the pain, in Imagination and Word ...

At this stage there seemed nothing to do but get out. That
this should happen in a liberated and socialist country!
Viewed from either Right or Left, I was always in the
wrong. I was feeling – we were feeling – totally unloved.
We went out that evening for a drink with a few faithful
friends, but exactly as we walked into the Coconut Grove
the gentlemanly news-reader of Radio Singapore began
yet again to utter the text of the 'unprecedented rebuke
issued by the Government of Singapore'. Back home, we
retired with sleeping pills, which were just taking effect
when the telephone rang. Muzzy and sore, I could only
make out that someone, some student or other, was inviting
me to comment on culture. 'You have a Minister of Culture
here – ring him!' was my uncouth reply. The next morning
I felt deeply ashamed of myself, for the caller was the
President of the University Students' Union, and he and
other officers had sat up all through the night preparing
for an Emergency General Meeting of the Union on the
following afternoon.

Either I was not totally unloved, or the Government was
not totally loved. Much to my surprise, and much more (I
would venture) to the surprise of the Government, over
five hundred students turned up at short notice to consider a
resolution which, without necessarily expressing support
for my views, condemned 'the Singapore Government's
attempt to strangle free discussion in the University and to
cow an individual into silence for expressing views which
do not coincide with the official ones' and demanded 'the
immediate withdrawal and cessation of such threats.'
Five hundred and twenty-two students voted for the
resolution, five voted against, and two abstained.

I was not so removed from the great world as to be unaware that it was a quite remarkable performance on the
part of the students and that the Government would have to
take cognizance of this distinct note of disagreement coming
from a notoriously apathetic, apolitical and coddled section
of the local youth. I began to think that after all one might
quietly and unaggressively stick one's heels in. Thus began
what became known as the Enright Affair, and I was to
derive a good deal of entertainment and enlightenment
from the hurrying events of the next few weeks. It was of
course a storm in a tea-cup, but one could observe in
miniature many of the currents and cross-currents, the
whirlpools and rocks, the beacons and the *ignes fatui*, which
feature in greater storms.

Somebody in the Government had miscalculated. The
people had reacted the wrong way. The offence was found
too slight – in the eyes of some no offence at all – and the
abuse too strident and vulgar for oriental stomachs. The
older and more traditional Chinese would feel that those
who, by the direct application of such terms as beatnik and
mendicant caused someone to lose considerable face, had
by their alarming disregard for face in effect lost face themselves. A local Chinese-language paper, while ticking me off
in a delightfully old-world style for my lack of manners in
referring humorously to sarongs and such-like traditional
appurtenances of the Malay minority, commented thus on
the Minister's letter: 'Some of the words used are damaging
to the professional status of the person concerned and give
the reader a most uncomfortable feeling. Other words have
yet to acquire common usage in the English vocabulary
and have no place in an official letter. All this may be said
to be of little import, but it does show traces of the impact
of emotion.' Yes, the Government would have been better
advised to hire a secret society thug to stab me quietly in a
side-street.

From feeling totally unloved I swiftly passed to feeling excessively loved for improper reasons. Opposition politicians

(yes, there were such in those days!) rang me to say how
long and dearly they had desired to make my acquaintance, and couldn't we get together now? David Marshall, a
celebrated fighting lawyer, who had been Chief Minister
of Singapore in the latter stages of the British régime and
was currently leader of the rather incongruously named
Workers' Party, urged me to engage him to sue the Government for defamation. He assured me that I should be awarded
I forget how many tens of thousands of dollars in damages,
though I would probably have to leave the State as soon as I
had collected them. He was sorely disappointed in me when
I declined his offer – 'So you won't stand up and fight?'
Having a medieval distrust of law and lawyers, I suspected
that it would end in my leaving the State sure enough, but
without the dollars. Moreover, I believe in fighting one's
battles in one's own way, and where libel is concerned I have
remained faithful to that maxim which says, 'Sue not, that
ye be not sued.'

I felt not the slightest temptation to yield to the blandish-
ments of Opposition politicians. I had conceived no radical
objection, hitherto, to the policies of the P.A.P., and was not
convinced that the party could be held to stand or fall by
an outburst of bad temper. It grew fairly plain that one
particular minister had run slightly amok, failing to consult
with his colleagues, and that (to recur to my Thai student)
the Prime Minister's heart was not in the sacrifice. (If he
had performed it personally, it would have been done much
more adroitly.) Furthermore I had on principle a good deal
of sympathy for the first indigenous government of an
ex-colonial territory. If I had forgotten I was a foreigner,
that was my mistake.

Support came from the oddest quarters and sometimes in
the oddest guise. The University Librarian went to the
trouble of ringing me up to assure me that, after the fashion
of Voltaire though she herself was a Christian, she abhorred
my views but would defend my right to express them to the
death. (Whose death, I wondered.) A drunken Indian

describing himself as a Communist (the first and last self-confessed Communist I have met here) took much the same line, abhorring my views, or what he took to be my views, only a little less than he abhorred the P.A.P. He appeared to hope that I would survive this storm so that he could deal with me more satisfactorily later on. (Four years later in the toilet of a restaurant I met a Eurasian who recognized me from contemporary Press photographs and told me that he had been on my side and wanted to write to me but dare not, because, he said, he was a Civil Servant. 'I still dare not,' he concluded, hastily fastening his fly and departing.) The boys behind the meat counter at the local supermarket told my wife that they had discussed the affair and were on my side, and they waved their choppers resolutely. When I went to the branch post office to send a reassuring cable to my mother in Leamington (alas, it had the contrary effect), the clerk was so touched by my oriental filiality that he went to some pains to work out the cheapest way of sending it. A cellophane box of orchids arrived at our house with an admirative note from 'Charles and Barbara': we never found out who Charles and Barbara were.

A number of the older Chinese in Singapore interpreted my remarks as a quite correctly low valuation of Malay culture and thus by implication a correctly high estimation of Chinese culture, and so I received a succession of benign and encouraging nods and smiles from that quarter. Letters poured in from all over. A very warm-hearted one came from a British sergeant stationed locally, asking how a Professor of English could be expected to carry out his duties properly if he were obliged to steer clear of local cultural issues. Letters also came from ex-colonial officers now back in England – for the Affair was covered by Reuters and widely commented on in the Press in England: it must have been the silly season there too – offering me warm sympathy and prudential counsels, generally to the effect that I should keep my own mouth shut but teach my students to open theirs; from the National Union of

Plantation Workers, with a request for an article on any subject of my choice for their journal; from a lunatic adherent of the theory that Bacon wrote Shakespeare, who somehow contrived to find confirmation of his views in the Affair; from someone who complained that he had anticipated the opinions expressed by me in an article which he now would not be able to publish. . . . There were also several highbrow begging letters or otherwise inconsequential communications, of which this will serve as a representative: 'I came across your name in the papers the other day in connection with a letter addressed to you from the Ministry of Labour and Law. I wonder, Sir, if you could kindly help me in assessing some twenty-eight poems which I have enclosed herewith.'

I received a cable from *Encounter* inviting me to send an account of it all, but this I didn't feel like doing, chiefly for reasons I have mentioned already and partly because I hadn't forgotten that a letter I wrote not so long before to Stephen Spender, concerning the Bangkok incident and the infringement of cultural freedom or whatever on the part of the British establishment there, had been returned to me on the grounds that Spender was away in America and shouldn't be burdened with extra reading. That, too, didn't seem a way of fighting this present little battle.

I was amused by some English and other foreign residents, who began by championing me stoutly against the unmannerly and bolshy P.A.P. (in private at least), and then turned on me when it looked as if I intended to stick it out in Singapore. They urged me to go, to leave in true sahib fashion, on my high horse. 'How can you stay on?' they asked, 'Have you no pride?' I suppose I didn't have any pride, at all events not the sort of pride that would be wounded by being called a beatnik, a mendicant professor, an alien, a bird of passage. In the world as it is these can claim to be epithets of something like honour.

·   ·   ·   ·   ·

Incidentally, on the day the *Straits Times* printed the first report of my lecture I had written to them in these terms: 'I note with interest that, under your own title, you have reported on the first fifth of my inaugural lecture . . . I look forward to reading your report on the remaining four-fifths of my lecture under its proper title, "Robert Graves and the Decline of Modernism".' The letter was published, but otherwise disregarded by the editor, and so six days later I wrote again, remarking that 'it would be nice if one of Singapore's newspapers – which seem to have space for their own version of my talk and for readers' letters about that version – could print the talk as a whole, as it was delivered.' The *Straits Times* then printed the preamble in full but nothing from the other four-fifths. They were interested neither in Robert Graves nor in the decline of modernism.

Meanwhile there was much activity behind the scenes as well as in front. One member of my staff, himself a local citizen, interceded with the Prime Minister, pointing out that I was not exactly constructed along imperialist-colonialist-capitalist lines. I heard from someone else, then a member of the P.A.P. but later to defect and be imprisoned, that when the charge of colonialist-mentality was obviously failing to stick, the party had for a moment considered switching to a charge of Communist allegiance; my informant claimed that he himself had disposed of this by reminding them that Communists went in for large families whereas the Yellow Professor had only one child. The printed form of my lecture was much in demand, orders poured in from overseas booksellers, and stocks were soon exhausted. And a beautiful girl came to whisper in my ear that I should stand firm, that I had well-wishers unbeknown to me, that there was a group of young activists within the P.A.P. who would be making themselves felt before long. (They did. The young men in question broke away to found the Barisan Sosialis, the Socialist Front, and before long they were nearly all put into prison, where some of them still are today.) If I had had any pride, I should have become puffed up with it.

17

Burying the Corpse

And here you stand
Scuffing the ground with your heels
Talking of freedom, and free to.
It's an unquiet grave.

LAGGING some distance behind the students, my fellow academics now got down to debating the Affair in their more judicial and judicious way. Two senior authorities had disappeared on fishing trips. But bodies met, views were sought and exchanged, and statements were not issued. For almost a fortnight it seemed to me that I was the only person in the University not totally taken up by the Affair. Like a model of conscientious dutifulness, I sat quietly in my office (I put in for a new air-conditioner and rather surprisingly got it), with the telephone off the hook.

The Academic Staff Association, a body which normally spent its time wrangling over terms and conditions of employment, called a special meeting, and (I gathered afterwards) there was a distinct feeling in some quarters that, while academic freedom couldn't be said to exist, the best way of perpetuating it was to throw the offending don to the dogs. This was to be the dominant academic attitude during the years that followed on every occasion when the University came into collision with the Government. Academics customarily possess such a gift for subtle reasoning and fine distinctions, such exquisite professional scrupulosity and verbal dexterity, that even an intelligent and shrewd observer may fail to perceive that much of the time their basic motivation is simple cynicism and self-interest. If you are in trouble, throw yourself on the mercy of the nearest peasant, publican or policeman, but never go to an academic: you will be dead long before he has finished formulating his attitude towards you and your problem.

There was one cheering aspect to these debates, I gathered: the split in opinion did not run between expatriates on one side and local staff on the other. But on the whole, however disconcerting the Prime Minister may have found the prompt and decisive action of the students (on which, in his shrewd way, he hastened to congratulate them), the behaviour of the rest of the University must have confirmed rather gratifyingly the contempt in which he held us.

The officers of the Staff Association, it should be acknowledged, did everything they could do in the difficult circumstances, and did it expeditiously. A deputation called twice on the Prime Minister to investigate the possibility of working out a formula of reconciliation satisfactory to the two parties primarily concerned. The Prime Minister couldn't seem not to be supporting his ministers, of course, nor for political reasons could he seem to be condoning my offence, even if he had felt inclined to do so. But at least he made some casually complimentary reference to me in the course of a speech at the annual dinner and dance of the Students' Union, while insisting that there was no question at all of academic freedom being threatened. The teacher could and should enjoy supreme freedom within his province – it was simply that his province did not extend to 'the heat and dust of the political arena'. (The proposition is less helpful than it seems when you remember that the political arena was the whole of Singapore. Mr. Lee's attitude towards the University, both before and since this affair, has vacillated between accusing it of being an ivory tower and instructing it to be one.) Mr. Lee finished his speech at the Union dinner by ascribing this storm in a tea-cup to bad reporting on the part of the *Straits Times*, a colonial-owned paper employing expatriate newspaper men. . . . It could be seen who was to provide the scapegoat ingredient in the prospective formula of reconciliation. I felt a little regret on this score – partly on account of a friendly letter I received from a leader-writer apologizing for the paper's failure to comment on the Government's rude letter and explaining that the risk was too great – but I can't say it broke my heart. The deficiencies of the *Straits Times* were by no means solely those of an honest paper compelled to bow to brute force; in the matter of the University Vice-Chancellor two years later its behaviour was jackal-like beyond the call of necessity.

The formula of reconciliation consisted of a public exchange of letters. I was to write a short, clear letter in simple language to the Acting Minister of Labour and Law, clarifying my position. Having approved my letter, the Minister would then compose a reply and forward it to me for my approval. The two letters would then appear simultaneously in the *Straits Times* and the 'vernacular' papers. My first letter was too long, too argumentative, explicatory and historical, almost another lecture, and so I had to write a second and more suitable one under the eyes of the officer-bearers of the Academic Staff Association:

'Dear Minister,

I shall be glad to elucidate some of the comments in the preliminary passages of my inaugural lecture on "Robert Graves and the Decline of Modernism", delivered in the University on 17 November and tendentiously reported in the Press.

In these introductory remarks I spoke of culture in general, meaning by that word "the production and consumption of art". In a local reference, I gave my view that, as a lively modern state and an open port, Singapore should remain culturally open, and thus gradually build up its own modern and appropriate culture. No sneers at Malay art or the Malay way of life as such were intended.

I can assure you that I have not the slightest desire to comment on or interfere in the political issues of this country, of which – as you have pointed out – I am not a citizen.

I remain, Minister,

etc.'

A copy had gone to the Prime Minister, the letter was approved, and it duly appeared in the Press. Despite the agreement, however, the Minister's reply went straight to the Press without my seeing it first:

'Dear Sir,

I refer to your letter of 23rd November in reply to my letter of 18th November.

If you had so stated your position at our first meeting in the afternoon of the 18th November, my letter to you would not have been necessary. But I am glad you agree that your status as a teacher in the University does not clothe you with the rights of a citizen to comment on or participate in the political issues of the country.

However, let me assure you that your right to teach your subject and to expound your views within your province of learning is completely unfettered.

Since my letter to you of 18th November has been made public, it would be necessary that your reply and this letter should also be published.

Yours faithfully,
etc.'

(English translation of Malay original)

One or two of the more sensitive officers of the Staff Association felt upset and guilty about this, but I was not surprised myself, for since the Government had more face to lose than I, so they had more face to save. And in truth it was just as well that I had not seen the Government's letter in advance of publication, for I might have felt obliged to point out that (*a*) I had not been given an opportunity to state my position 'at our first meeting', with its faint but still perceptible odour of rubber truncheons, and (*b*) I had straightaway, by means of my letters printed in the *Straits Times*, indicated the tendentiousness (as I saw it) of the initial reporting. But then, as Kipling said:

Men who spar with Government need, to back their blows,
Something more than ordinary journalistic prose.

The Affair continued to rumble on in the Press, spurting
up from time to time. Readers' letters were roughly in the
proportion of one for the Professor (or more often against
the Government's harshness) to three against the Professor.
This probably wasn't due to tendentious selection by the
editor, though it didn't coincide with my personal impression of the state of opinion. The adverse letter-writers either
believed that I was seriously advocating more and louder
juke-boxes, or complained that (though they themselves
could see what I was trying to say) I had wantonly wounded
the feelings of thousands of other people, or were alarmed
lest I should be encouraging the students to claim more
freedom than was good for them. Mention of the Affair was
generally accompanied by a rather unfortunate photograph
which with difficulty I placed as having been taken soon
after my arrival, exhausted by Indian literary and spiritual
exigencies, in the bar of the York Hotel, the hotel where I
spent my first week in Singapore. It was undeniably the
picture of a man who, when he heard the word 'culture',
reached for his bottle of beer. Much later on I bumped into
the wife of a cabinet minister at a University party, and
she told me that what had set her against me at the time was
not what I had said or the Government had said (she didn't
take any of that very seriously) but my brutal sneering face
as featured day after day in the *Straits Times*. Mind you, I
had been let off lightly, as I realized during the period of
'Confrontation' when the *Straits Times* regularly printed a
photograph of Soekarno which gave him an insane wolf-
like visage with long needle-sharp fangs. In such small
but telling ways can a newspaper aptly demonstrate its
loyalty.

But the Affair was essentially dead, and all the Government wanted was that it should be buried too. The last

person left to defend the Minister of Culture with much
conviction was – or so one of the P.A.P.'s bright boys told
me – some middle-echelon member of the staff of the
British High Commission in Singapore.

18

The Lytton Strachey of Singapore

TO take up that old question, just for the sake of argument – why did I stay on? In the first case because of those 522 students who would have been left looking rather silly had I promptly departed, whether abjectly or in sahib's high dudgeon. But I never, after the first hours, saw any over-whelmingly good reason for leaving.

Others did and still do, right up to today, seven years after-wards. Periodically, though with decreasing frequency, I am assaulted by local citizens apparently hostile to the P.A.P. who inform me with considerable vehemence that I ought to have left the country as a matter of principle. If my departure could possibly have resulted in the fall of the P.A.P. and the rise to power of a better-tempered, more affectionate, more liberal, internationalist, academic-freedom-respecting régime, then I would agree with them. But I haven't observed, with the possible exception of Jesus Christ, that absence from the scene has ever proved a great positive force for good.

And I must admit, the Enright Affair had aspects which I found amusing, congenial, even invigorating, up to a point. There was a degree of legitimacy about the Government's action if not about their phraseology. It is not so dreadful to be taken seriously, even if one is not altogether correctly understood. If the British took poetry seriously, then the Typists' Union would have come out in protest against Part III of *The Waste Land* as constituting a gross misrepresentation of the members of the profession and their personal habits. Naturally we would mock at them, and we would have to put them down before they managed to bring out the entire clerical staff of Messrs. Faber & Faber. But at least the incident would show that somebody had read the poem seriously. Where literature is concerned, perhaps a back-handed com-pliment is better than no compliment at all.

Moreover, I am a great believer in the saying about the preferability of words to sticks and stones. The Minister of Culture didn't actually clout me. The action of the Government appears to me even endearing when compared with the action and inaction of my compatriots on and after the occasion in Bangkok which I have related. I do not recall that, after that episode, anyone urged me to carry my distresses to some liberal-minded British M.P. or renounce my nationality. The Singapore business took place largely out in the open (would it now, I wonder?), whereas the Bangkok affair was closely huddled up in a series of visits to offices and little chats in the best diplomatic manner. If the former was characterized by unparliamentary language and hot air, the latter had a cold sliminess about it which was much nastier.

I must seem to have taken far too long over this trivial episode already, and the reader may well resent having his nose rubbed in these dried turds of village history. A storm in a tea-cup indeed. Yet fortunes are told in tea-cups, and I still think the affair is worth dwelling on for its exemplary interest. And so I append a few notes for political scientists, the morticians of our age, on the hidden factors, the unvoiced considerations behind the Affair. Thus, (a) the charm of knocking on the head an interfering foreigner, even more potent when he is a member of the outgoing power; (b) the implied rebuke or threat to the English-educated section of the populace: stooges of the colonialists, effete, apolitical, complacent, reaping-what-they-had-not-sown . . .; (c) a step in the P.A.P.'s largely lip-service promotion of Malay, the language, whether stripped or not of its cultural ethos, as a preparation for some sort of merger with the Federation of Malaya, a part of the sustained attempt to make Singapore and its large Chinese majority look acceptable to the Malay politicians north of the causeway. In the event, (a) the charm failed to communicate itself to the populace as a whole; (b) the English-educated took nervous note, muttering how odd it was that

the Prime Minister and the Professor had been to the same
English university; (c) the Singapore Government's gallant
defence of Malay culture cut very little ice up north, for some
Malay leaders confessed to their own ignorance of what Malay
culture could be, apart from praying five times a day and
observing the fast of Ramadan (incidentally two procedures
which hold little attraction for the average Chinese), and
others, however appreciative of the P.A.P.'s solicitude, must
have found in the intemperance of the Government's outburst confirmation of what they already expected from a
Chinese-dominated socialist-infidel régime.

   During the following six years a number of expatriate
teachers were to be dislodged, in one way or another, for one
reason or another. Some because they were difficult to get on
with (one doesn't expect this from foreign guests) or not
especially competent (if you are going to import an expert,
then he had better be an expert), others because they were too
clever or too articulate in their insistence that academic matters
should be ruled by academic principles and not political
considerations (the vulnerability of this argument lay in the
sad fact that whereas the academic principles appeared to be
foreign imports, the political considerations were undoubtedly home-grown). The process of dislodgment was more or
less quiet (for one thing the *Straits Times* had lost its taste for
academic coverage), taking for instance the form of general
discouragement or thwarting in small professional matters.
The financial rewards were not so splendid as to compensate
for the petty unpleasantnesses, new universities were spring-
ing up everywhere, and the largest staff migration was to
Australia.
   The Government was not seen to be acting or directly
acting in these matters, it didn't want any more idiotic
scandals, for it was clear that foreign investments were needed
and that, if cause for alarm were given, firms thinking of
opening up would move over to the milder atmosphere of

K

Kuala Lumpur and its suburbs. If nationalism seemed to be the policy for internal use in welding the races together, then it needed a bland exterior if it was not to unnerve foreign businessmen. This consideration was all the weightier after 1965 when Singapore was going it alone.

The faint odium, the odour of official disfavour attaching to the Professor of English, lingered on, but now at bureaucratic rather than Cabinet level. Civil Servants have long memories; and this is a fitting retribution for petty trouble-makers – to be sniffed at by clerks. Radio Singapore (a division of the Ministry of Culture), for whom I had done several jobs prior to my disgrace, now dropped me and left me dropped for six and a half years. Recently they invited me to do occasional book reviews for the radio, but after due reflection I declined on the grounds that both Radio Singapore and I had got along quite nicely without each other for so long that there seemed no point in changing our lack of relationship. At some stage in the years between I happened to meet the Head of Broadcasting at a large party and, being more than usually relaxed, he confided that he had often received suggestions that I should feature in radio programmes, but alas, it was more than his job was worth to bring me back. I am not implying that this was any loss either to the public or to myself; there was plenty of canned professional stuff for the former, and as for myself, the fees paid by Radio Singapore hardly covered the tax and the petrol used in getting to the studios. I mention the matter not out of resentment nor in hope of extorting commiseration from my reader (who by now, I trust, will not be too quick to lavish sympathy on me), but simply because it happened – and because it is a neat, though trivial, illustration of how a cowed bureaucracy continues to promote with zeal what it supposes to be its masters' policies long after the masters have lost interest.

Another and more disquieting instance of this was the reluctance of the immigration department to renew my annual work permit on its first expiration, in February 1961, a reluctance either to renew it or to state an intention not to renew it. For a while I was illegally resident in Singapore, and being by nature law-abiding, I pointed this out to the authorities. Their reaction was to offer me a month's extension of stay, which I rejected as a vulgar piece of back-street bargaining. I was friendly with a young activist in the P.A.P., who later broke away, was detained, released and banned from the state, and now lives happily and unpolitically in the *bourgeois* capitalist country of Malaysia – a life-cycle which goes to show that you can be too far Left for a Leftist régime and still get on well under a Rightist régime, and also that mere or sheer personalities still count even in the most highly developed and doctrinal of political societies. On investigating the case, my friend found that the question of the work permit of the Professor of English had been passed from one official to another, each delaying the matter because unwilling to commit himself to a decision. My friend mentioned it to a minister, who looked puzzled, then said, 'Routine case. Renew it, of course!' The message passed swiftly down the bureaucratic ladder and into the ear of the man at the bottom who kept the rubber stamp.

My symbolic status was to last for a long, long time, well past the point at which I grew sick and tired of it. I had come to feel fraudulent and ashamed. So much so that in July 1966 I felt compelled to write to the *Straits Times* begging for remission of symbolism:

' According to your account of the University of Singapore's forum on university autonomy and academic freedom, Mr. X Y [*a young lecturer in the Law Faculty*] alluded, in somewhat ritualistic fashion, to "The Enright affair". That "affair" occurred almost six years ago, and if those concerned for university autonomy and academic freedom can find nothing more recent or more serious to discuss, then the relations between the University and the Government must indeed be happy.

In fact most people have forgotten what "the Enright affair" was about. I am frequently saddened, at cocktail parties for instance, to hear about someone bearing my name, who apparently

got into obscure trouble with the authorities long ago, and has
since left the country, or died – or at any rate has done nothing
either before or since to justify his existence. I am sure the P.A.P.
would not wish to be remembered solely in connection with
"the Enright affair" – any more than I would wish to be remembered solely as the other protagonist in that rather ludicrous
business.

Academic freedom and university autonomy are worth fighting for, I believe, because if they are not fought for then they will
go by the board entirely – to the detriment, in the long run, of
the University, the students and staff, and the country. But
they should be fought for on firm and on firmly remembered
ground. They are real, and not – what "the Enright affair" has
become – mythical.'

This letter was not too well received by some of the younger
local staff of the university (including Mr. XY) and I was told
rather snappishly that I wasn't exactly helping these young
fighters for academic freedom. Once one had acquired symbolic standing, however reluctantly or unworthily, one just
had to grin and bear it for the public good. I could only
answer that any plea for academic freedom, or (unwise in any
case, this!) any campaign to persuade the Government to
draw a specific line of demarcation between the properly
academic and the improperly political, which invoked the
Enright affair would be pretty promptly and easily dismissed
by the Government on the grounds that the Professor was an
expatriate. He who pays the piper calls the tune, and not so
long before the Government had threatened to close the
purse-strings, just to see what would happen at the end of the
month when the salary slips failed to turn up . . . In these circumstances, you fight for freedom, good, but not for freedom
for *foreigners*.

In truth I felt that the concept of academic freedom had
become identified with me to such an extent that much worse
threats (and worse than threats) to academic freedom and even
offences against academic decency arising in other quarters

had been ignored. When I suggested this I was told that I was wrong, I was told that these other incidents were compli- cated, obscure, bedevilled by this and that, lacking in the clear classic simplicity of the old Enright Affair . . . I had never myself considered the latter so especially simple or clear, but I could see that it now had the advantage of being essentially dead, and was thus a convenient arena for a little shadow- boxing.

Nearer the mark perhaps, or less sadly off it, was the director of the Political Study Centre in Singapore, a sort of high-level propagandist agency set up by the Government primarily to instruct or rehabilitate the civil service. Its (British) director had earlier been Public Relations Officer and then director of Information Services for the colonial government of Singa- pore, and he was undoubtedly a trustworthy, versatile and extremely competent Civil Servant. As once presumably he had taught the beauties of British colonial rule, now he was promulgating the glories of nationalism. In 1962 the Political Study Centre arranged a series of lectures which school- teachers were bidden willynilly to attend, the chief object being to instil a sense of national consciousness into them. The director himself gave a brief history of events since the de- parture of the British and, I gather, declared that the present time, characterized by a necessary puritanism, could be com- pared with the Victorian age in British history. The Professor of English at the University, now . . . he should not be taken too seriously, for he was an irresponsible iconoclast, one who criticizes for the sake of criticizing . . . as it were, the Lytton Strachey of Singapore . . . The lecture was followed by a period of free discussion in true democratic style, and on this occasion a recent graduate from the English department had the temerity (she was a woman, and temerity seems to come more readily to women than to men) to ask the director whether he knew what the Professor had actually said in his lecture and whether he disagreed with it. The director was quite a good sport, and confessed that he didn't know the Professor personally – he might well be quite a nice man, really – and hadn't actually read that lecture of some eighteen months ago.

Iconoclast? What idols had I sought to smash? Surely not the deodorized plastic Muse of the P.A.P., multi-coloured yet sombrely grey, multi-lingual yet seemingly dumb? Not that I myself had any objection to the description. Considering its dormancy in the art of *belles lettres*, Singapore might be held fortunate to be able to point to such a late literary manifestation. And I suspect that the senior members of the Government would not have objected too strenuously to being thought of as Eminent Victorian *de nos jours*.

In 1963 or 1964 a dissident political group operating outside the country pirated a poem of mine called 'Prime Minister'. The poem itself was harmless; indeed I considered it a not unsympathetic general study, applicable to almost any Prime Minister of any newly independent country who finds himself under the necessity of issuing orders for the arrest of the young men so recently his comrades in the struggle against the imperialist power. But when the poem appeared in a propagandist sheet put out by dissidents and reputed subversives, it inevitably seemed less than sympathetic towards one particular Prime Minister. Yet the Singapore Government took no steps against its author. For one thing, the poem had originally appeared in an Australian journal, and it seemed that there was an agreement between the Government and myself – it must have been a gentleman's agreement since I was not actually aware of having entered into it* – that I

---

* I only became aware of this useful agreement in July 1965, when Singapore was part of the federation of Malaysia, and the Central Government in Kuala Lumpur expelled Mr. Alex Josey, a British journalist living in Singapore, for engaging in local political activities outside his brief as a foreign correspondent. Mr. Josey had been working as Press relations officer for the Prime Minister of the State of Singapore – that of course

would not publish matter critical of the Government in any *local* periodical. Lest this should seem a grave delimitation of cultural freedom, liberty of expression and so forth, I had better mention that to my knowledge there was not at this time any local periodical which would dream of printing anything likely to offend the Government. And, in case this should look like a piece of offensive irony on my part, I had also better say that there were very few local periodicals at all.

But the Prime Minister, as agile as ever, turned the incident to his own advantage. In one of his speeches, delivered (I believe) to the university graduates' association, he dwelt on the growth in maturity achieved by his party since coming to power in 1959. 'Now we can even allow the Professor of English to write his poems.' The remark was received with applause and appreciative laughter from the audience. Most of them had of course never read a single line of the Professor's, and now they knew they needn't bother to.

was the gravamen of the objection to him – and so the State Government was duly enraged over this illiberal action by the Central Government. Some people had opined that the State Government's indignation rang a little false since what the Central Government had done to Mr. Josey was no different from what in pre-Malaysia days the Singapore Government had proposed to do to Professor Enright. The Singapore Minister of Culture then published a long letter in the *Straits Times* (it hinted *en route* that, as an employer of non-citizens, the paper was asking for trouble in apparently endorsing the Central Government's action) to the effect that both his Government and Professor Enright had conformed faithfully to the ruling which had it that I was not to comment locally on local political issues but which 'has not prevented the Professor writing articles and verses critical of the P.A.P. Government in journals abroad.' Mr. Josey's work in Press relations did not amount to political activity, he maintained, and Mr. Josey had also published only abroad – yet, unlike the Professor, he had been expelled. The story has a happy ending, however – a month later Singapore left Malaysia and Mr. Josey flew back into Singapore.

19

A Servant of the People

Whatever work they put me to, I will endeavour
To be of use to the country. That is my purpose.
If on the other hand they hinder me with their systems –
We know how clever they are: shall we talk straight? –
If they do hinder me, it isn't my fault.

CAVAFY

LEAVING behind the 'dust and heat of the political arena' into which I had absent-mindedly stumbled – rather like Svevo's Zeno walking out to find roses for his daughter and inadvertently crossing a new military frontier – I now retired to the peace and quiet of the ivory tower. For, as I have mentioned, though reproached for not entering into the real life of Singapore, the university had discovered that it was likely to be reproached more severely if it dared to encroach on the real life of Singapore. And so to cultivate my own garden, my English garden, and to pursue the role of the good expatriate, who presses on with the job diligently and quietly, without getting his name into the papers. Like, say, some faithful senior clerk to Sir Stamford Raffles, or a humble, foot-slogging and uncomplaining havildar. Rearing up those who would in time render me superfluous (except that they generally landed jobs more attractive than mine); sometimes consulted by such august bodies as the Ministry of Education (generally after they had decided what course of action to adopt); very often consulted over the phone or by letter (the ivory tower is not without doors and windows) about English syntax, vocabulary, grammar, style and idioms ('Dear Sir, I am a clerk and I am having a row with my employer who says that "dispose it off" is not correct expression in English. Will you please write and tell him he is wrong'); and

occasionally writing something about the country for magazines overseas, though only after I had ascertained that no
local citizen was prepared to accept the commission and that
if I didn't do it, it wouldn't be done at all, which (I felt) would
be a pity . . .

Yes, I have endeavoured to be of use to the country, and the
less I was required to be useful, the more I desired to be so. I
will not here adduce the teaching of English literature (or the
organizing of other people to teach English literature), because this has been held to be a dubious service if not a dis-
service, and because I shall be speaking on the theme later.
But I cannot refrain from mentioning the masses of literature
I have read and to the best of my ability commented on, verse
and prose, ranging from the epics of old Indian ladies whose
eyesight is failing to the gloomy riddles of young Chinese or
Malay boys whose spelling never succeeds. In my inaugural
lecture – alas, so widely read and so literally construed! – I
had declared that 'to obtain art, you must leave people free
to make their own mistakes . . .' So I could hardly object when
people took this as an open invitation to send me their own
mistakes. And all the less when, from time to time, I would
come across successes or promises of future success; I was
amused to find that by 1964 or so I had formed a higher
opinion of local writing than that held by the Minister of
Culture, which gave me to wonder whether I hadn't caught
the bug of nationalism, albeit that of a nation not my own.

Once you swallow your pride – a process more or less
difficult according to the size of your gullet and the size of
your pride – there are all sorts of things you can do to help a
new or emergent country on its way. As I write, I am about
to give a reading of my own poems (if approved by the police)
at a charity concert, very appositely too, since the proceeds
will go to retarded children. I have even done the Singapore
Police some small service. In 1965 a young police inspector
was killed in the course of a pitched battle with a gangster.
The latter had barricaded himself in a room and for several
hours he kept at bay a large raiding party of police, killing the

inspector and wounding two other officers before he was shot to pieces. (The gangster, a Chinese, had the odd alias of 'Morgan', by the way.) Later on the editor of the *Police Magazine* wrote to me asking if I could provide a poem in memory of the inspector for printing alongside a prose obituary: 'the poem should be one befitting the sacrifice and as such we feel that the best person to approach would be yourself.' Now the police had been extremely kind to me, in patrolling the house regularly while we were away, and I would have liked to oblige them in return. Moreover, like anyone else, I felt sorry for the inspector's family. But as well as being unexpected and touching, the request was rather embarrassing, for I felt miserably sure that however I tackled the job the gangster would finally emerge as the hero. Looking through some old poems I found one which I had written in the early hours of the Enright affair some five years before, a distastefully self-commiserative piece to the effect that in the midst of life you are in danger. It struck me that with a few small changes, notably among the personal pronouns, and with the insertion of a pertinent reminder that should danger strike it was no use pleading family responsibilities, the poem might be felt to have some indirect but decent bearing on the event it was intended to commemorate.

My advice was that if the editor wished to use the poem then it should appear unsigned, since it was not a personal tribute but meant to express the feelings of the inspector's colleagues. In a seductively modest reply, the editor gave his opinion that the poem ought to be signed, since no one would suppose policemen to be capable of producing such poetry. I reiterated my opinion, but assured him I would accept his decision on the point. I was relieved, though, to see when the magazine appeared that the poem was attributed to Anon.

I had discovered in myself a small but distinct talent, or perhaps only a predisposition, for the writing of obituary verses. Now had it been the *closing-down* of the British Centre in Berlin ... When in 1963 the University's Vice-Chancellor, Dr. Sreenivasan, was forced by the Government to resign (for, in brief, showing the qualities and pursuing the policies which one would expect of a Vice-Chancellor) I printed a poem about the affair, in *Encounter*, chiefly because it was the only way that those of us who were saddened by Dr. Sreenivasan's treatment could get anything into print about it. A letter which my friend Ernst de Chickera and I sent to the *Straits Times* was not printed. (De Chickera, a Ceylon-born British citizen who had taught for the past eleven years in Singapore and was at this time Dean of Arts, had been advised by the Prime Minister, speaking through a respected member of the local Ceylonese community, either to keep his mouth shut or else go back to Ceylon and tell *them* all about academic freedom etc.) And when in later years senior officers of the university reproached me gently for publishing items which might create trouble for them, I would make bold to promise them that, should they come to grief, I would compose obituaries for them too.

I note with some uneasiness that a few days ago, in a fit of abstraction, I wrote my own obituary. But then, after one's memoirs, what else is left to write?

A further small service which I did the State was in what might be called *The Case of the Bulgarian Daughter*.

Singapore was in the process of establishing trade relations with Bulgaria, and in mid-1966 a Bulgarian Commercial Counsellor arrived in the country and opened an office. It appeared that the Counsellor had a daughter of university age with him, and she desired to enter the University of Singapore to study Economics and English, with the intention (it later appeared) of following in her father's footsteps. What was inconvenient was that she desired to take the three-year courses leading to a degree in these subjects. She had missed the first term of her first year, because some undesignated Singapore official had misled her father as to the date of the commencement of our academic year, and since by Bulgarian law she was not permitted to remain abroad after her father's return home, she would need to be granted exemption from this first term.

Another question was whether she was eligible for admission at all, in view of her (to us) exotic and unassessable educational qualifications. She held a Bulgarian school-leaving certificate, with the grades 'Very Good' in Bulgarian, Russian, Mathematics, Physics and Chemistry and 'Excellent' in Bulgarian History, Bulgarian Geography, Biology, English and The Principles of Communism. She had also taken an advanced course in which she had obtained either 'Very Good' or 'Excellent' in Astronomy, Electrical Engineering, Mechanics, Physical Training and Shorthand. In Bulgaria she would have entered a Science faculty.

A local student with such an educational background would never be admitted into the university, let alone granted exemption from the first term. Indeed a local student with such a background would be promptly admitted into gaol. But though local students needed to produce a Suitability Certificate (the negative result of political screening) before applying for admission to any institute of higher education, the Bulgarian Daughter, it appeared, enjoyed diplomatic immunity. It was quite in order for her to be a Communist.

Senate referred the question of her admission to the Arts Faculty. While such was formally proper, I felt that in this particular case it was passing the buck, and I stated my opinion that if she were admitted it would constitute a singularly gross instance of a foreigner obtaining concessions which would never be granted a local applicant, and also that her having missed the whole of one term's work made it very doubtful that she would pass the first-year examination in English.

A certain Professor Z then spoke. Professor Z, originally an Englishman, was a member of the P.A.P., indeed an adviser to the party, and he was popularly supposed to be the leading Government spokesman in the university – or, as he himself once put it in the delightfully frank way of those whom frankness cannot hurt, the P.A.P.'s 'Trojan Horse'. Professor Z, in his customarily dire tones, now declared that it was

absolutely imperative for the country to develop trade relations with Bulgaria and that, if anything should harm those
relations, then Singapore's economy would simply collapse.
In my pedantic fashion I tried to argue that it might be less
harmful to international amity to reject this Bulgarian
Daughter at once than to admit her and have her fail at the
end of the year, which was only some five months away.
Mrs. Z, the Professor's wife and also a member of Senate,
intervened to tell us but how exciting, what a new experience
it would be, to teach a young person from an entirely different
culture, and how one ought to welcome this marvellous
opportunity, etc. But neither Mrs. Z nor Professor Z was
going to have to teach this young Bulgarian person, unhappily; and as for myself, who was, I was having quite
enough trouble already with culture and cultures.

In a hurt, weary yet long-suffering manner, Professor Z
pointed out that he was only concerned, as ever, to preserve
the university, to prevent yet another disastrous collision
with the Government, and that if I, Professor Enright, was
to be instrumental in keeping this young lady out of the
university, then I must make it plain to the Government and
the people of Singapore that it was indeed I, Professor Enright
personally, who was responsible and not the university . . .
And true, the Head of the Economics department had mani-
fested no doubts or hesitations.

When the next afternoon the matter went before a special
meeting of the Arts Faculty, I kept my mouth shut. Faculty
is a rather honest and comparatively innocent body of predominantly young people, and it seemed best to keep it that
way. Faculty decided that the candidate could well be admitted as a non-graduating student in the first instance.
Wisely – wisdom out of the mouths of babes, indeed – the
second instance was left to look after itself. Had Faculty rejected the application, the Vice-Chancellor could and no
doubt would have over-ruled us and admitted her on his own
prerogative. It would thus have been easy for Faculty to
preserve its honour, had it seen the matter in this light,

by passing the buck to the Vice-Chancellor, so easy as to be pointless.

Despite this dark and muted epic of threats of catastrophe and tragic responsibility, no one seemed in the least interested in the Bulgarian Daughter once she had been admitted, this young person lost in a strange culture. It fell to me to introduce her to the Library, the lecture rooms, the exotic *mores* (tutorials and essays) and the toilets. In all I gave her some fifteen hours of extra tuition on the first term's work in poetry and drama. For if she failed the examinations now, it would surely seem sheer vindictiveness on my part – or what, in this context, is known as 'expatriate provocation'. But alas, I had the dubious consolation of finding my pessimistic expectations confirmed.

The part of the drama course she had missed was concerned with *Antony and Cleopatra*, a play whose issues were utterly incomprehensible to her. The poetry course dealt with the English seventeenth century and it inevitably involved sex and God, two subjects which her Bulgarian schooling had not touched upon and which apparently her own nature had no inkling of. Not that sex posed much of a problem – it was God who was the trouble. Donne and Herbert and God. It struck me that there was a world of difference between someone like myself, born at a time when God was ailing seriously but still alive, and someone like her, who had come upon the scene well after His confirmed demise. It was not merely that she couldn't believe in God, but she couldn't for a moment believe in anyone else's believing in God. Zlatina was a nice girl, friendly, wholly unaggressive and willing to please, and far from stupid, but while she had nothing personal against either of them, she was not going to pretend that anything which had to do with God or the After-life could be other than totally boring because totally irrelevant. There were churches in Bulgaria, she told me in response to my anguished probing, but they were patronized only by very old people. She herself had visited one or two, in order to inspect the architecture. ('As some to church repair,' I cried out happily,

'Not for the doctrine, but the music there – Pope – later this term!') She spent most of our tutorial sessions in politely, even apologetically, shrugging her well-developed shoulders. Love (shrug) Roman responsibilities (shrug) lust (shrug) Serpent of old Nile (shrug) Go and catch a falling star (Astronomy? No? shrug) To his Coy Mistress (shrug) To God the Father (shrug). I couldn't decide whether by local standards she was a hundred years old or ten years young.

If the future of Singapore depended upon Zlatina passing the examination in English, then it seemed painfully clear to me that Singapore had no future. There was also the minor question of the future of the English department . . . It was a Singaporean on my largely expatriate staff who suggested that the Bulgarian Daughter should be passed round the department for tutorials so that, when she failed, the whole staff would be held responsible and not me alone.

Perhaps it was that that did it. Or perhaps, as the syllabus came nearer to modern times and God diminished in presence, she found the work more congenial. Dickens, for instance, she knew something about him, and about Wordsworth, that old revolutionary. At all events, her examination papers, which were marked without concession, brought her an unambiguous pass. In fact they were much like everybody else's. I was still a little surprised, but glad. She had worked hard, and I like to think that the staff and students of the department had done something to make her feel not utterly alien.

But when the Faculty Board of Examiners met, it turned out that Zlatina's only clear pass was in English. History – which she had chosen as the required third subject for the first year, to be dropped thereafter – had warily given her a conditional pass, that's to say, a fail which could be considered a pass if she passed in her other two subjects. But in Economics she had obtained a very bad, wholly unambiguous, fail.

Zlatina was on holiday in Bulgaria when the results came out. She did not return. Her father, the Counsellor, went along to the Registrar's office and bawled out the junior official responsible for despatching the results: the mark in

Economics was incredible, it just could not be, his daughter was a hard worker . . . We heard nothing more. Singapore did not collapse economically. By this time the country had also established trade relations with Rumania.

Happening to meet Professor Z much later, I asked him whether he was acquainted with the sequel to the Case of the Bulgarian Daughter. He was not, and he obviously wasn't interested in the least. This did not deter me from telling him how gallantly the English department (albeit staffed largely by expatriates with no stake in the country etc., unlike the Economics department) had striven to ward off national disaster. He was merely bored by my story. It appeared that while it was all-important at *that* time that the Bulgarian Daughter should be admitted to the university, it was a matter of no importance that she had failed so miserably in Economics at *this* time.

And so the Case of the Bulgarian Daughter ended happily after all. Happily for the national economy, happily for the university, and happily for me, since at Christmas, shortly before the beginning of the examinations, the Counsellor had sent me two bottles of Bulgarian wine and one of Bulgarian champagne. My staff suggested that these gifts should be distributed among them so that the guilt of acceptance might also be shared, but I drank the champagne and gave the wine to a recently released ex-political detainee living across the causeway.

It ended happily for everyone, except Zlatina. And I hope that she is now happily studying Bulgarian Science. Here we await the Case of the Rumanian Son.

20

Reflections of a Non-Political Man

MOST books about Eastern countries fall into one of two categories. On the one hand, the factual, statistical, political-scientific or sociological, which makes everywhere sound like the inside of the same university senior common-room and gives little idea of the specific *taste* of life; on the other hand, the travelogical, impressionistic, patronizingly congratulatory, full of quaint customs and ancient instances and what my Thai student would call local technique colours, apparently aimed at elderly people who pride themselves on not reading fiction and have no intention of travelling to foreign parts. The former category of books usually fails to tell any living truths, while the latter sometimes succeeds in telling a lot of interesting lies.

Except (as one would expect) in the case of Japan and the Japanese, the majority of books in both these categories are written by outsiders. And it is not to be wondered at that in some new countries literary discussion has grown a new dimension and the question 'What is the writer's nationality?' takes precedence over 'Can this writer write?' Perhaps the nationalists are right, and books written by foreigners cannot help but be inaccurate. One waits for the nationalists to write their own books.

Naturally this nationalist theory will thrive, if only briefly, in lands where a sense of nationality is devoutly desired and largely absent. In one of its applications it received a boost some little time ago in Singapore as a result (as so many things are) of some seemingly casual remarks passed by the Prime Minister. The subject was expatriate teachers, and in simple terms (eager helpers soon reduced it to those) the theory could be summarized thus: the (let's say) British teacher, however good a teacher he may be in England, becomes a bad teacher when transplanted to another country, because, no matter how

well he knows his subject, he cannot by definition really know
the students he is teaching. One is aware of the element of
reasonableness about this proposition; one is even more aware
of its seductive charm for those in the profession who like
an empty ladder in front of them. While the expatriate
teacher or writer may feel it unseemly to offer to contend
against such theories (for not all will have my thick skin), he
will at least have the satisfaction of observing that no *good*
local teacher or writer will be found to exploit them.

'How can you presume to write about this country when
you have never lived in a Malay *kampong*?' True. So one
waits outside the *kampong* for the books to emerge. But *kampong* dwellers, it would seem, have better things to do than
write. Furthermore, books get you into trouble – yes, this is
one thing that illiterates know about books! Better leave
books to foreigners, who can always beat a hasty retreat . . . I
must admit that I find the morals of this matter so complicated – or so complicating, as they say in Singapore – that I
have failed to arrive at any formula more subtle than: Whoever you are, wherever you are, publish and be damned.
That is what a writer is for, it always was, and it always will
be.

As British officials move out, so American experts move in.
Nature abhors a vacuum: throw one foreigner out and ten
new ones come in. Each new country, in its babyhood, fathers
a new academic subject, a new department, a new library, and
a set of new specialists with sabbaticals and travel grants in a
score or two of universities. And no doubt many books about
Singapore and Malaysia will have been published before these
amateur reflections of mine see the light of day. Even though
both countries, and especially Singapore, are abnormally
difficult to write about readably, because there are so many
reservations to make to one's generalizations, so many bits of
mere or sheer information to be conveyed, that the footnotes
are likely to squeeze out the text. The difficulty with Singapore is aggravated by the fact that the P.A.P. is a more than
usually *political* party. Nothing is too trivial for it to take

note of, as we have seen.* And while it would appear to have great respect for and take great relish in ideology, it is quite ready to shift its party line whenever circumstances or supposed circumstances would seem to advise. The upper structure of the party philosophy on examination bears a strong resemblance to an encrustation of the *bons mots* of Mr. Lee Kuan Yew. And he is extremely witty. While we would not expect scholarly monographs to bear the signs of blood and and tears, the political studies I have seen of Mr. Lee Kuan Yew's Government are exceptionally remote in manner, almost as if they were respectful obituaries or measured accounts of the more or less worthy doings of some king who lived and died a hundred years ago. Perhaps this is due to the difficulty of catching a moving subject, perhaps it is due to caution, perhaps it is due to something else. The saying that every country has its own brand of science is certainly true of political science.

.   .   .   .   .

'I know the style you have got used to in power . . . In your young middle age you have achieved your style. You are without emotion, but you have your ideas. You are clean, spare, dedicated men. Each face gives you back the same image of the world. You speak your own language, clipped and dry, for you have absolute power, in the turn of a paper, and the untidy language of men is forgotten, shut out, beyond the guards at the door.'

(*Koba*, Raymond Williams)

In this brief question and answer section, the questions are profound.

* One contributory factor in the formation of a separate association for local staff members of the University of Singapore – or so many people will tell you – was the complaint made by some citizens that they could not speak at meetings of the old Academic Staff Association without expatriates spitting pointedly. The culprit was later – but too late – found to be an expatriate Chinese with sinus trouble who was under the necessity of clearing his passages at regular intervals.

What is Singapore?

An island of 224·5 square miles, inhabited by a little under two million people, of whom approximately 79 per cent are of Chinese stock. The largest minority is formed by the Malays (12 per cent), followed by Indians and Pakistanis (6·6 per cent). The island is now a republic, with an elected government (its leaders mostly Chinese) and a President (Malay). It is linked with West Malaysia (earlier 'Malaya') by a causeway across the Johore Straits.

Why did Singapore leave Malaysia?

Why did Singapore go into Malaysia in the first case? Despite the autonomy provided for in education and labour matters, the conditions attending its entrance were still rather humiliating – fewer seats in the House of Representatives (15) than were allotted to Sarawak (24 seats, population 780,000) or even to Sabah (16 seats, population 475,000), while at the same time there was a wide-spread impression that the over-riding reason for bringing Sarawak and Sabah in was to prevent the Chinese predominating numerically. (In Malaysia as eventually constituted they comprised 42 per cent of the population.) P.A.P. leaders have always been particularly sensitive to anything resembling humiliation. Did they then really believe that Singapore was not viable by itself?

When in mid-1963 the London *Times* was preparing a special supplement to celebrate the inauguration of Malaysia, I was invited to contribute a colour-piece on the life of the peoples of the new federation. I felt I had to decline, partly because of insufficient acquaintanceship with the various peoples, but partly too because I felt my account would be coloured in a quite inappropriate sense by a feeling that the federation wouldn't work. The feeling was intuitive, un-reasoned, but if I had to give reasons I suppose I would hesitate a doubt as to whether Singapore's Big Brother was really reconcilable with Malaysia's Big Daddy; the easy-going tolerance of the Tengku, the prince, who wanted his people to enjoy themselves, with the passionate intensity of Mr. Lee

Kuan Yew, the lawyer, who required his people to justify themselves; the fierce didactic ideology of the Chinese politicians with the folk-wisdom of the Malays.

As it turned out, the extremists on both sides proved too much for the moderates, and even sooner than anyone more reasonedly sceptical than myself would have expected. And the pity of it was that, politicians aside, and racists, religious fanatics and rabble-rousers discounted, the two regions were humanly more or less continuous, and their inhabitants by nature amenable to reasonable compromises on most questions arising in the course of everyday life. It must be granted that in saying this we have pushed aside and discounted quite a lot!

Malaysia was to be a nation, with a national consciousness. To achieve a national consciousness, you must have something to create it *against*, in contrast *with*. Obviously it won't do to pick on one of the races or cultures present in the country as a model of what should be and leave the others as models of what should not be. Thus, in a grimly humorous sort of way, the secession of Singapore helps both Malaysia and Singapore, for now each can seek to define itself nationally by reference to or against the other. Earlier the separateness of Singapore and the States of Malaya was attributed to the cunning imperialist policy of Divide and Rule; the successors to the colonial power now see some virtue in the policy of Rule and Divide. If the leader of one country praises peacefulness, the leader of the other will extol the military virtues; if one leader exhorts his people to taste the good things of life, the other will warn his people that they had better be prepared to tighten their virtuous belts; both leaders must be in favour of multiracialism in all things, but each can complain that the other is insufficiently multi-racial . . .

A sense of nationhood is procured, it seems, only in the context of an external threat. When your nearest country is just on the other side of a short causeway, the threat has the advantage of being near at hand, so near that those foreigners can easily walk into your country and take work out of your hands. Nationhood is more readily acquired through fear and distrust of others who are 'different' in some way from you than through love and trust of your fellow citizens who can't be quite the same as you since they are bad drivers, go in for marathon bouts of noisy 'Chinese opera' or muezzins who cry out arrogantly at all hours of the night, keep savage dogs, are a charge on the parish, etc., etc.

So far hostilities have been limited to ministerial asides and, more significantly, the sphere of visas and work permits. Those Singaporeans who talk cheerfully, with a sort of relish, of graver trouble to come are forgetting that graver trouble would mean shooting bullets at Uncle X in Johore Bahru and setting fire to the house of Second Sister Y in Kuala Lumpur, for if the nation is to be greater than the race it will also have to be greater than the family. Nationhood requires tigers. In this case the tigers will have to be paper ones – but good imitations.

For months previous to the establishment of Malaysia the schoolchildren who form an unusually large percentage of the population of Singapore were rehearsed in a catchy little jingle:

> Let's get together, sing a happy song,
> Malaysia for ever, ten million strong . . .

The children liked the tune and had gone to some trouble to learn it and so after Singapore's secession they amended the text slightly:

> Malaysia for ever, ten minutes long . . .

Although Singapore is a mere village in comparison, I cannot help but think of Fielding's remarks on India as a nation in Forster's novel. 'What an apotheosis! Last comer to the drab nineteenth-century sisterhood! Waddling in at this hour of the world to take her seat!'

Can Singapore survive?
Foreign experts, at least when speaking privately, seem to

think not – the republic is not viable, economically, militarily, politically . . . I think, or rather feel, that it will survive, short of course of some cataclysmic event which will affect the whole world hardly less drastically and not much later. Because it will have to. Because it is to other people's advantage that it does. Because the Chinese are experts in survival. And because the people of Singapore are not in the mood to go down; since they cannot decline gracefully, they will have to stay up. I will admit that some of the qualities I most admire in them are qualities which it appears are now to be discouraged and reduced. For instance, their individualism, their scepticism, their distrust of politicians, their loyalty less towards 'the State' than towards family, small groupings and individuals, and their natural inclination to take outsiders as they find them.

These characteristics are not among those which go to make a nation, and the Government desires to make a nation. Thus a sophisticated populace are to be trained as soldiers, not necessarily for the sake of fighting a future war, but because military training is a swift method of inculcating discipline and because, in the words of the Foreign Minister (formerly Culture), 'when young Chinese, Malays, Indians and Eurasians train together and work together to defend and die for their country, then they become true blood-brothers.' War games do hold out a certain attraction for some of the sophisticated, even though they may have been brought up to feel that good iron isn't used for making nails nor good men for making soldiers. But then, they are to be gentlemen-rankers. However handy a military establishment may be, both in swallowing up gangsters and in absorbing the better educated who might otherwise drift into political subversion, the Government (as civilian intellectuals) will not be unaware of the danger inherent in creating a disciplined professional force which could be turned against it.

The Government is at present taking the line that what the country needs is not pigeon-chested bookworms but healthy, disciplined young people imbued with the team spirit, and (following the Prime Minister's gaze) the Ministry of Education is turning its eyes backwards and westwards to the public schools of Britain. My view, for what it is worth, is that healthy, disciplined young people, runners, jumpers and weight-lifters, are a luxury which the country can afford precisely because of its pigeon-chested bookworms. A country of under two million *needs* mandarins more than warriors.

Recently some young school-teachers, many of them women, were being drilled, and seeing that they were English-educated, the Malay army instructor thought it would be nice to vary the language of command and tell them to stand at ease in English. 'Open all legs!' he shouted, and wondered why discipline suddenly collapsed among the young women.

What sort of a Singapore will it be?

Chinese, but less and less China-orientated. Chinese education used to carry greater 'cultural' prestige, but increasingly English education is seen to have, still to have, greater career value; the Chinese here are unlikely ever to forget they are Chinese, but they will remember it less frequently.

Not a nation perhaps, because it has too high a proportion of thinking persons; nations need a solid and stolid base of stupidity and sluggishness to found themselves on; but a small and reasonably independent and materially prosperous island.

Much depends upon Lee Kuan Yew, of course, and what happens inside him. Tough, energetic, realistic, intelligent, shrewd – these are the adjectives most commonly used of him by foreign commentators – of local commentators there are so remarkably few that one might almost suspect an element of dumb insolence, but more probably it is the oriental reluctance to define that-which-is lest one should thereby tempt providence to change it for the worse. Just as benign, tolerant, fatherly and well-loved are the adjectives generally given to his opposite number in Malaysia. For Tengku Abdul Rahman has the qualities Mr. Lee is deficient in, and *vice versa*.

Mr. Lee is a born leader, with only two million people to

lead and, seeing how well-off they are relatively (often the adverb is unnecessary), with nowhere terribly exciting to lead them to. The vision he must hold before their eyes is more often the black picture of what may come about if they do not give him their whole-hearted support. The record of his Government in material matters is an excellent one, notably in industrialization and the provision of cheap housing. In moral or spiritual matters it is less impressive, for so far its favourite method of teaching people to stand on their own feet has been to knock them down to begin with. They are to be threatened into virtue, to be browbeaten into virility and sturdy independence. They are urged to be 'politically aware', to take a greater interest in politics, while they observe that those who were politically aware and ambitious to be sturdily independent of the P.A.P. were soon removed from the political scene. The nearest approach we have at present to sturdy independence, it seems, is the sight of a Government back-bencher rising to ask a question to which the front bench have the full and authoritative answer.

The Chinese are what some Germans lately claimed to be – internal emigrants. They do not recognize any sense of honour which requires that their public behaviour should always conform to their private opinions. They are docile because they are prudent, and because they are sceptical as regards such grand abstractions as freedom and independence. In his book *Chinese Looking Glass*, Dennis Bloodworth remarks that before a Chinese starts righting wrongs and fighting good fights he must remember that if he ends up in hospital or gaol or the grave he will have betrayed his family and 'his good deed will earn him the well-deserved disapproval of all decent-minded people.' But Mr. Bloodworth's book also demonstrates that the Chinese is docile only up to a point: push him beyond that and he will bite back quite fiercely.

At present Mr. Lee is too easily contemptuous of others, and it is no excuse to say that he has often been given good reason to feel contempt. I once compared him to Saturn, a man of power who felt obliged to destroy his progeny by

swallowing them. I doubt whether Mr. Lee would have the
stomach to swallow some of his latter-day collaborators and
admirers. The toughest, most rugged of his younger followers
were the men he detained or banished or otherwise forced out
of politics, and now he must patrol the schools, demanding
more foot-drill, more running, more press-ups, more of an
uncomfortable and obscurely useful exercise called burpees.
Sacrifices, we are told, will have to be made (and true, there
seems scope for sacrifice in some quarters), but of what? The
sacrifice of double book-keeping? Of half of next month's
salary? Of the teacher's mini-skirt in exchange for teachers'
uniform? Of scholarships to Britain and the U.S.A.? And
sacrifice for the sake of whom or what? Some nervous souls
might think gloomily of Brecht's lines –

> *Those who are certain to gain by the offering*
> *Demand a spirit of sacrifice.*

Mr. Lee was born out of his age. He is a hero in an anti-
heroic age. He can hardly rest content with the vulgar practice of raising the Communist scare – that tattered old alibi
for the iron fist. (We are told there are Communist activists
on the university campus. Dutifully we look for them. We
fail to find them. Exactly! For we are then told that this is
because firstly real Communists are too clever to show themselves and secondly we are too stupidly liberal to recognize
them if we saw them.) Instead of leading the charge with sabre
raised at the front, Mr. Lee is forced to pore over economic
statistics in a back room. To be a Coriolanus and have to stand
in the market-place displaying one's wounds is bad enough –
how much worse to be a Coriolanus in a country which is one
large market-place!

In our day nature's heroes tend to turn into environment's
shrews. If they are prime ministers – especially if they are
prime ministers of countries so small that they can be very
nearly everywhere at the same time – they may find themselves running their fingers along the tops of classroom desks
and waving the result under the noses of terrified headmasters;

or, by way of their Education ministries, warning principals and teachers that if they hope to gain promotion or to avoid disciplinary action 'they should refrain from patronizing bars of dubious respectability, where waitresses encourage customers to flirt with them'; or delivering a speech against male university students who have conducted a 'panty raid' against a female students' hostel (deplorable of course – I hasten to state that I hold no brief for this pursuit – but scarcely calling for action at prime-ministerial level); or complaining that ceiling fans have been left on in Community Centres when no one was there ... Acknowledged legislators, yet they beat their all too effectual wings in a void. The spectacle may amuse outsiders, but it is truly sad and a little alarming.

'Each man kills the thing he loves,' Wilde remarked in one of his less glittering but more humane moods. And he defined the cynic as 'a man who knows the price of everything, and the value of nothing.' The two sayings go part of the way towards describing what the hero who lacks an heroic part to play can turn into. Happily these days there are lots of high-level international conferences to keep our masters occupied, and unlimited opportunities for theoretical derring-do, for engagement and disengagement.

As for Mr. Lee, along with a taste for exercising them, he possesses in a high degree those lesser talents so necessary to a modern statesman, of brilliance in exposition, agility in argument, a sharp eye for his opponent's weaknesses, and a seeming spontaneity. Perhaps there are still sufficient fields for him to conquer, and the curse of petulance, as of a bad-tempered Achilles sulking in his domestic tent, can be averted. He might content himself, if not with the quantity, then with the quality of his people, reminding himself that a good deal of what he disapproves in them arises from the vices accompanying the virtues he values most.

21

What became of What-was-his-name?

Andrea: Unhappy the land that has no heroes!
Galileo: No, unhappy the land that needs heroes.

BRECHT

I don't know whether M— could be said to be one of the
sons that Saturn swallowed.

At that time Secretary-general of the Singapore National
Union of Journalists, he was arrested in February 1963 along
with 110 others, in the course of a pre-Malaysia round-up
wittily called Operation Coldstore, and in mid-1967 it was
announced that he would be deported to Ceylon once it had
been established that this country would take him. He was
born in Ceylon, but came to Singapore at the age of two or
three and in due course took local nationality. It was just his
bad luck that there happened to be somewhere, a birthplace,
to which he could conceivably be deported.

I was told that he would have been released from detention
and permitted to stay in Singapore had he been willing to do
as many had done before him – publish a recantation of his
former Communist views, appear on TV and declare that the
scales had now fallen from his eyes and he could see that
Singapore's present mode of government was more natural
and appropriate. I was told that he refused to do this on the
grounds that since he had never been a Communist he could
not renounce that creed. Friends sought to persuade him to
make the gesture nonetheless, to understand that honour and
policy, like unsevered friends, could grow together. Four
years lost from his life – surely that was enough?

But he obstinately insisted on staying in gaol. Did he perhaps think of himself as a martyr? His friends told him he
shouldn't deceive himself on that score for, far from being

remembered as some sort of hero however crazy, he was hardly remembered at all in Singapore. As evidence of this someone adduced a poem called 'What became of What-was-his-name?' which I had published in *The London Magazine*:

> *Funny,*
> *After three years*
> *A new generation hangs around the place,*
> *Hardly one of them has heard of M—.*
> *It makes you feel your age . . .*

The argument backfired. But somebody has written a poem about me – he answered – so you see, I am not forgotten.

Not for the first time I felt a twinge of moral discomfort. Yeats had wondered,

> *Did that play of mine send out*
> *Certain men the English shot?*

Times change, and poets and poetic effects with them. All I had managed to do, it seemed, was to encourage a man to stay in prison.

I cannot speak of M—'s views or of his activities before arrest,

> *But he must have done something very bad.*
> *The papers said nothing about it.*

Security considerations require that there should be no public discussion of the activities of those arrested for the sake of preserving security. We do not know, for we are not told, whether a detainee has imperilled the whole country or irritated a member of the governing party. How naïve it was of our former Vice-Chancellor (no wonder he had to go!) to tell us in Senate again and again that justice must not only be done but must be seen to be done. There are occasions in our world, it seems, when justice can only be done as long as it is not observed in the process of being done. The Vice-Chancellor's scrupulousness was matched after his fall, when some of my more scholarly colleagues objected to a memorial motion expressing our full confidence in him because (as they pointed out) the word 'full' presupposed a fuller and more intimate, continuous and exhaustive knowledge of his actions than any of us could possibly have had. The motion was passed as soon as the loose word was elided.

After a man has fallen from grace it is easy to find good reasons for his fall. Good reasons, that is to say, for not associating oneself too closely with him. When we read literature or history, we hate the villain, we despise the traitor, our hearts go out to the brave man and the innocent victim. Then the same situation arises in life, in the present, and we hasten to adduce those 'special circumstances' which will honourably permit us to respond quite differently from the way we responded to the story in the book. (And then we read the story of *this* in a book, *this* story. But it doesn't change matters one jot. For the splendid thing about special circumstances is that they are always *special*.)

Not, as the poem scrupulously admits, that I ever knew M— well . . . But, whatever the truth may be, I think his fate can serve as an epitome of the condition of the liberal in the world as it is. The Communist is accustomed to a party line and to obedience and to the idea of public confession. Unless he is a pure fanatic, he doesn't find it overwhelmingly difficult to change his line from Communism to anti-Communism; and having recanted, having faced the mild ordeal by television in which he will play the hero as much as the villain, like a backward boy, previously despaired of, who has suddenly passed all the examinations, then often he will serve his new masters well. But the liberal, the man who believes in truth and justice, or in fairness and decency, he cannot be trusted. He is the enemy of all doctrine – it was his sort of person who said 'there is no general doctrine which is not capable of eating out our morality if unchecked by the deep-seated habit of direct fellow-feeling with individual fellow-men' – and every politician's hand will be against him. His politics were shifty to begin with and they will continue to be so. He sees good in practically everything, he sees bad in practically everything; he grants you your point, and then expects you to grant him a point in return. He cannot be relied on, he is undisciplined, unrealistic, ungrateful, and he pampers his little private conscience. Prison is his proper place.

22

Students Again

A few words about students again, about Singapore students, or about Singapore viewed through its students.

A reluctance to come to grips with the literature itself, with
the text, is nothing unusual among students all over the world,
nor among teachers of literature. Nor is the reliance on 'the
critics', the retailing of the opinions of other people, of the
authorities. Yet there is a sense in which Singapore students
are rather different from others: the word 'retailing' is more
than commonly apt. They have remarkably shrewd – even
alarmingly shrewd – minds, a top layer of speculative in-
genuity which leads one to expect a layer of deeper reasoning
and feeling which is not always there. Though if you grow
accustomed to not expecting these depths, you will miss them
when they are there, of course.

Singapore students read widely among the critics, in a
business-like spirit, shopping around for a 'bargain' judgment
or a second-hand interpretation with some wear left in it.
They are far-removed from the (perhaps mock-modest)
spirit of 'a poor thing, but mine own'. Only the best is good
enough for them, and the best is generally to be found in
Leavis, Eliot, Yvor Winters, Bonamy Dobrée (usually accent-
less), Cleanth Brooks, Grierson, Derek Traversi, G. Wilson
Knight and L. C. Knights (whom they find an inconvenient
set of un-twins – aggravated by the pseudo-triplet, J. Dover
Wilson – and tend to telescope into one Shakespeare Critic),
and the *Pelican Guide to English Literature* (including, on the
War Poets, myself, whom they incline to treat in gingerly,
somewhat formal fashion, as if not quite convinced that this
printed authority and their all-too-human teacher can be one
and the same) ... However, there are always one or two auto-
didacts who return with treasure acquired inexpensively in
the international thieves' market – Freud, Jung, Ernest Jones,

Wittgenstein, Stopford Brooke, George Saintsbury, Sartre, Schopenhauer, A. C. Bradley, *Nineteenth Century Fiction*, the *Colorado Teachers' Journal* . . .

Another peculiarity of student attitudes here (something you would hardly ever come across in Japan) is the curious relish they take in finding fault with authors, the petulance they display towards a poet who has committed some small error or is guilty of a minor lapse of decorum. We had to drop courses on Practical Criticism in the first year because the students took to the exercise all too zealously, often, in Dr. Johnson's terms, finding themselves barely able to establish the point of precedency between a louse and a flea, or else warily covering their bets and finding there was 'something to be said' for everything, but not very much for anything. It is as if an author has already put himself in the wrong by being an author, so that any punishment which follows is deserved and justified without the need for more than the shadow of a trial.

Admiration tends to be grudging, at the best. Donne has certain praiseworthy qualities – that is, at least he is better than something else, in this case the simple-minded Elizabethan lyricists who preceded him and placed women on a pedestal (for some reason it is the women students who are especially contemptuous of this practice) – but then 'he goes too far'. When I am dead and opened, I think you will find the words 'he went too far' carved in my heart. Examples of 'going too far', if examples are actually proffered, often seem curiously arbitrary – such as the poet loving his wife excessively, or actually begging God to batter his heart. Thus the poetry of the First World War was distinctly superior to what came before, because at any rate it was 'down to earth', whereas those pitiful Georgians were all at sea. But then Wilfred Owen, having began so promisingly, 'went too far' and spoilt things by using disgusting imagery like 'a devil's sick of sin'. In a first-year examination script I marked, the candidate declared that it was quite understandable that Macbeth should murder Duncan (anyone might have done the same) and he had his reasons, and good ones they were, for killing Banquo too. But when it came to the murder of Lady Macduff and son, 'Macbeth has gone too far, he has forfeited my sympathy.' Claudius went a bit far: 'though the last King has died but two months ago, he has already married his widow and stopped all mourning. This is surely against court etiquette.' Pope, too, went too far, he 'exaggerated', he compared a lady author to a cow. The odd thing is that this comes from students who at other times can face the most violent and cruel literary invective without turning a hair!

In part this distaste for excess arises out of a deep-seated gentility, a gentility which is mostly confined to public matters such as social behaviour and literature, for in personal encounters these young people are generally remote from the genteel as we know it in the West. In part it is the same attitude which we noticed in Thai students: authors, and poets in particular, are impractical people, they *do* tend to go too far, and they are to be accompanied for only part of the way. About some things poets are far too simple, idealistic, 'unrealistic': in other matters they are far too complicated, 'far-fetched', unrealistic in the other sense.

Returning to Macbeth, Singapore students show next to nothing of that horror of regicide evinced by Thai students. Of course, they have no king of their own, they never had one, and they lost their overseas emperor some time ago. Their attitude is more pragmatic: if you kill a king, you are likely to be found out – or, at the best, a worse king will succeed. Their censoriousness towards Antony has little to do with his tumbling on the bed of Ptolemy, but much more to do with his inability to tumble on beds and simultaneously win in battle. 'He was too old for that sort of thing, and so was she' – they should both have rested content with military and political prowess. Sex they take in their stride, and the tiniest, shyest and most fragile-looking of maidens will show no embarrassment during the explication of the grossest sexual allusion. This is a phenomenon which might upset some teachers (the students *ought to be* embarrassed or shocked, there must be something wrong if they are not), but I have come to consider it altogether admirable, since I have no wish (I am thinking of George Steiner's remarks on guiding students through *King Lear*) to take into my hands the springs of their being. They are neither tap-water nor plasticine. And literature – for I am pragmatic too – is meant to add to what is already there, not to take away or to pervert or corrupt.

The students who get round to reading Henry Miller, Frank Harris or *Fanny Hill* nearly always find them boring – boring because grossly incredible or (as they put it) 'unrealistic'. These books 'exaggerate', they 'go too far', therefore they are of little value. Similarly cool was the attitude of a girl student who had a bet with another girl on where exactly in *Sons and Lovers* (a first-year text) Miriam lost her virginity, and came to me for a verdict. She was being realistic.*

Again, their attitude towards *The Waste Land* and similar modern works is the very opposite of the Japanese attitude. The Japanese maintain – or used to maintain ten years ago – that the Waste Land *was* Japan. Tokyo first, and afterwards London, Paris, Vienna and so forth. I think the peculiar attraction of the poem for the Japanese is or was by no means an *après-guerre* phenomenon alone, but something more basic and permanent than that. But Singapore students enjoy Eliot's poem and in response write long essays happily lambasting 'modern civilization' for its commercial-mindedness,

* The police, on the other hand, tend to be prurient. The 'English' theatre in Singapore is entirely amateur, and the texts of plays chosen for public performance must be scrutinized by policemen. In recent times the police have objected to the words 'virginity' and 'hot lust' in *The Women of Troy*, to a reference to 'a shaker-full of martini' in William Inge's *Picnic*, and to the line 'birth, and copulation, and death' in Eliot's *Sweeney Agonistes*. On appeal and explanation the first two of these objections were withdrawn just before the curtain went up (it transpired that the affronted officers supposed that the shaker-full of martini, being enjoyed in the back of a car, was an exotic American orgy-technique), but 'birth, and copulation, and death' had on pain of closure to be changed to 'birth, and procreation, and death', a substantive amendment, just because a senior police officer (though prepared to allow the word once) found himself having bad thoughts on its fifth appearance.

its triviality, its lustfulness, its over-all degeneracy. For them all this happened somewhere else, it is essentially *foreign* history. They do not for a moment identify the departmental secretary who rebukes them sternly if they come late for tutorials with the girl of the drying combinations. The Japanese react tragically, the Indians also, but Singaporeans react Confucianly: literature is exhortation or admonition, and therefore you expect it to be 'exaggerated' or 'melodramatic', with incredible whites and impossible blacks. This is not a bad reaction after all. For – to change Johnson's meaning a little – if you were to read *The Waste Land* for its story, you would hang yourself!

Returning to their petulance, one only wishes that an artistic triumph could arouse such intensity of personal feeling in them as does (it seems) a minor defect. But then, as I have suggested, they *expect* the best as a matter of course. If it is felt that this attitude is a strange one to find in a recently liberated people, who grew up cowed and spiritually under-privileged beneath the imperialist yoke, then I can only agree that it is indeed a strange state of affairs – but a real one. They expect the best, only the best is good enough for them, and hence their indignation over the imperfect condition of the goods occasionally offered by Donne, Marvell, Milton, Pope, Wordsworth and so forth.

It is impossible not to feel a pang of sympathy for Mr. Lee Kuan Yew, as he strives to make a virile, rugged, fighting little nation out of this collection of urbane and spiritually affluent individuals. I would myself feel a greater pang if I were not, through a timidity of nature, disinclined to total admiration of virile, rugged, fighting nations. The curious thing is that people who calmly expect the best quite often do get it, and if you have a gift for placid and unobtrusive assurance, much of the time your life will be a placid and assured one. Why work out your own responses to a literary work when you can take over some professional's response? Why keep a dog and bark yourself? Why build up an army when somebody else can arrange to do whatever fighting proves necessary? (Moreover, as one can see from the papers, soldiers tend to go too far.) Why engage in politics when you have politicians all ready to engage for you? Why aspire to be a hero when the cemeteries of the world are full of the bones of heroes, not to mention those who didn't get a proper burial. (He who lives last lives longest.) Why desire a history when histories are the record of disasters and suffering? If your grasp falls short of your reach, then what's a heaven for? – it can't be for *anything*!

If at times the contemplation of the attitudes of the people of Singapore drives one to tears, more often it leaves one in a state of stunned and slightly resentful admiration. Though (outside the arts) they may not have great expectations, not great romantic ones, yet they have certain expectations. They combine the stoical inwardness of the East with the sociably relaxed exterior of the West. Westernly progressive, they approve of family planning; Easternly philoprogenitive, they approve of babies. In a Western way they believe in ideas and creeds, symposia and forums; in an Eastern way –

> *To die for one's own belief*
> *What is it, but murder*
> *By one's child?*

– they believe in survival. Honesty, they judge, is the best policy (Singapore rates high among foreign businessmen who resent having to yield up part of their profits in the form of rake-offs elsewhere in Asia), as being both the most profitable in the long run and the least arduous. Life holds no mysteries for them – and yet they can still go on living, and what's more enjoying life, for the young are properly and decently young and the old are properly and decently old, so that whatever their age may be, it always seems to suit them. No, this won't do. We can't have this. We had better call in the human engineers and weld them into a nation, aware of their responsibilities, cognizant of their duties, in full realization of their role, conscious of crisis, and so forth.

23

Loose Ends

ONE day our old Bangkok landlord passed through Singapore. Not old in himself, indeed a young Australian-trained architect. He had been away at the time of the punch-up in the lane, returning to find to his astonishment that his tenants had flown. However, the British Council representative called on him to explain matters, and chiefly to explain that his late tenant was a nice man really but given to drink, which had proved his downfall.

'I told him,' said our good-hearted ex-landlord, 'that I had never seen you drunk. Drinking, yes' – in moments of stress he would come across to us for a restorative whisky or two, as when his dog, uninoculated against rabies, bit our daughter, or when he heard that Marshal Sarit's wife had been given the contract to design a new military base – 'but not drunk.' In righteous indignation he had gone to his brother, a senior policeman, and between them they had contrived to have the brothel closed down. 'Very difficult,' he said, 'It was owned by a princess.'

I could well imagine that it would be difficult, in fact I expressed my surprise that it could be done at all. I was a little alarmed for the landlord, who was given to spasms of idealism but seemed doubtfully cut out to be a St. George.

He explained that his elder brother wielded a certain amount of influence in the force because he was celebrated for his incorruptibility. Years back other officers had tried to get him dismissed because of this unorthodox quality, but Marshal Pibul had declared himself against the idea – there ought to be room in the service for one honest officer, he had declared, if only to set a standard.

Our landlord confessed sadly that the brothel was currently open once more. But when he got home he was going to do his best to have it closed again. 'I shall not give in!' I couldn't

feel a very vivid interest in this campaign of his. If anything
were to be closed down, then I would have liked it to be the
police force – or better, certain foreign missions.

· · · · ·

> *Within a week, the Master*
> *Touches sweet oils to virgin canvas,*
> *And makes three paintings.*
>
> *To be hung,*
> *To be chatted up.*
> *And maybe bought.*
>
> *Perhaps he even serves the State,*
> *Even that perhaps –*
> *Who can prove the contrary?*

What has happened to the national culture which was to be
brought about in Singapore? That too, in a way, has been
closed down, opened up, closed down, and opened up again.
It was of course from the outset a political concept with a
simple political objective: to homogenize a very mixed
bunch of people, and thus make them more amenable to
living together, working together and being ruled together.
It was not, that's to say, primarily to do with the enrich-
ment of their personal lives, with the refinement of their
individual sensibilities. *That* – as politicians are wont to say
of things they despise or cannot comprehend – could come
later.

I was not so surprised as some other people when a few
weeks after my inaugural lecture and the ensuing row a
report appeared in the paper of an address by a safe second-
echelon P.A.P. man on culture, in which he appeared to have
said just what I had said, minus the particular and pointed
allusions. 'Openness' after all is not really a thing to be
objected to in a society where each racial community suspects
the others of ambitions towards cultural domination.

Subsequently the Minister, a conscientious man, made

various speeches, about the desirability of contracting mixed marriages (a proposition to which the older people nod assent, and then hope devoutly that their own children will marry within the race), or how the rubber-tappers ought to have their own folk dances. There was a good deal of talk about writing and what it ought to be and do, but very little writing. In these circumstances, writing was at the best an ambiguous operation, for it involved the choice of a language and by implication the rejection of the other three main languages of the region, thus accentuating division rather than stressing togetherness.

Nor was music much better, it seemed, for little could be done with this art except for concocting *pots-pourris* of Chinese, Malay and Indian styles, which mostly sounded like the music for an undistinguished Hollywood film about the East, and wasn't especially popular with that sizeable public whose natural liking was either for Beethoven or for the Beatles. Painting, quite obviously, was an art of which much more could be made. Understandably it is the most prosperous of the arts here, so far the only one which can hold its own at the international level. Exhibitions are many, and they are generally opened by a Minister or a Member of Parliament since these constitute what we have by way of 'public figures'. The celebrity will inevitably speak of the particular exhibition and of painting in general in terms of his own occupation. While – the more wittily, the higher his standing in the party – he discourses on the contribution of the artist to a multi-racial society or the development of a national consciousness, the painters stand around smiling faintly. They are glad to hear that they are fulfilling such an important function, even though they were not conscious of it at the time. The weaker vessels among them tend to exploit 'the oriental' (and these do well out of what can be called the tourist trade). The work of the better could often have come from Paris, New York or London. Naturally we like to detect local influences or tendencies, and so we point to the influence on the painting of some young Chinese of the Chinese ideogram, though it could just as well be the influence of the girders of the Forth Bridge.Why should he object? If people are to buy you, they must be allowed to talk about you.

Painters, probably because they think with their brushes and not with words, are sensible people, less vulnerable to the theories and desiderations of politicians and the excogitations of political go-betweens. They have a decent pride, they don't feel continually obliged to justify themselves and their vocation. They are even, without having to make a special effort, regarded as respectable members of society. They are lucky.

Writing in English appears to be finding its feet at last. It is bound to have an element of the 'exotic' about it, legitimately; for one thing it will use an admixture of words from the local languages, not deliberately, not for the sake of 'local colour' as a selling point, but because these words are commonly and naturally used in everyday life. Nonetheless the danger of running into the ludicrously macaronic remains. For the language of these writers *is* English, and alas they have entered into competition with the *Oxford Book of English Verse* and its centuries – just like any other English poet. They will have to decide whether they wish to be judged by 'absolute' (that is, literary) standards or by special 'local' standards. The world will urge them to choose the latter, to partake of that new phenomenon, that new 'subject', administered fairly legitimately by sociologists and anthropologists and ignobly by careerists, called 'Commonwealth Literature'.

One deficiency which all creative work suffers from here (outside university poetry-writing circles, perhaps!) is the absence of informed and relevant criticism, though this is better than suffering from an excess of professional criticism. The criteria, here as in so many other spheres, have been political, political and political again. Just think of these new countries, born straight into a smog of politics! Their case is very different from the older countries: at least we came

trailing clouds of glory, we took time in polluting the atmosphere of our lives. We grew up surrounded by other
things, with a richer diversity of values in the air – religion,
morality, art, philosophy. Largely because of our literature,
we were blessed with a wide range of vision, it was at least
possible for us to grow up unblinkered. But in the new
countries everything from the beginning has been 'political'.
This was not by choice exactly, for it was the older countries
who invented blinkers and then exported them, yet it
probably owes something to the fact that the brightest men
to emerge in the new countries were nearly all politicians.
Perhaps the essential fault of the University of Singapore
was not that it was ineradicably suffused with 'the colonial
mentality', but that it assumed without thinking (and
perhaps this is what 'colonial mentality' sometimes means)
that there were other values and other activities than
political, and that politics were a means to an end rather
than an end in themselves.

What is to be deplored is not the absence of 'pure'
criticism, the disregard of 'aesthetic values', so much as the
crude and oppressive presence of political standards, so
powerful and yet so protean. And something persists which
is healthier or at least hardier than academic standards or
aesthetic values, and that is a distinct (if generally unvoiced)
scepticism concerning political attitudes and judgments in
artistic matters. There is a remote region in the soul to which
politicians have not yet managed to secure unfailing access,
and people do have an inkling that there is something better
to be had, something wiser, something older, which politics
can interpret, perhaps use or abuse, but not replace.

We noticed that Buddhism has been held an obstacle to
the writing of great poetry because it offers a solution to
every conceivable problem and removes every reason for
outcry or rebellion. It is, by this account, a vade-mecum and
panacea, and hence all tears are by definition idle and the
heart cannot break, except through weaknesses that no one

would wish to boast about or from causes so illegitimate or childishly unreal that no one would care to set them down in print.*

But of course not every man is a Buddhist, nor every Buddhist as absolute as this. And the paucity of writing in some Asian countries which we regard as belonging to the Western or anti-Communist bloc should have attracted more attention than it has. I mean, it ought not to pass un-remarked. We certainly take note of the exciting words which arise from time to time on the other side of the Iron Curtain, and of the dire noises of strangulation which some-times follow. We do not consider the silence which reigns among some of our acknowledged allies. Yet surely that silence signifies something?

As far as I could tell, while a number of writers in Thailand were turning out polite novels of social life, amiable stories about amiable people, there was very little poetry being written other than the pietistic (praising the Buddha for removing the necessity for poetry) and the strictly personal (love poetry, but far-removed from that 'detailed description of the sexual act' adumbrated by the student).

The paucity of writers in Singapore and Malaysia to date is to be ascribed to a variety of factors. The region is multi-lingual, and inevitably (at least until the language laboratories break through the sound barrier) each language is hampered by the coexistence of the others, so that the writer is nowhere intimately at home, and in addition the reading public is sadly fragmented. These are natural or at any rate historical causes. But there are also causes less natural. Writers observe that they are not taken much note of until suddenly and dis-concertingly they may be taken too much note of. You can

---

*And this situation has been dealt with, briefly but definitively, once and for all, in one of the most famous of all *haiku*, written by Issa on the death of his only child:

> *The world of dew*
> *Is a world of dew and yet,*
> *And yet.*

be surer of the final kick than of the initial ha'pence . . . The comfiness of anti-Communism, the intellectual gentility which it fosters, is apparently as lethal to writing as the omnisufficiency of Buddhism.

Writers and would-be writers in some Asian countries are under the impression that they will get into very hot water if they publish anything which someone or other construes as politically objectionable. Have there in fact been any cases of victimization in Singapore or Malaysia? No doubt an occasional civil servant has been warned by a nervous or jealous superior that if he hopes to prosper in his chosen career he had better watch his pen. This hardly amounts to persecution or governmental brutality! But what matters is that, rightly or wrongly, intending writers are *scared* – the atmosphere they feel is hostile, and they are not reassured by (say) the broadcasting official who looks at a poem, lifts his eyebrows and says, 'Well, I don't know about this . . . It will have to be cleared by someone higher up,' giving the poet a cold look, as if to ask why on earth can't he be content to produce stuff that isn't controversial. Like the eternal verities . . . By a sad paradox it is exactly those who call for a local literature who have done most to discourage local writers.

It is true that in the countries I have just named there hasn't been a genuine test-case. No one wants to be a martyr, no one wishes to jeopardize career and family for the sake of a poem or an essay which might not even be a good poem or essay. A man writes a poem in Chinese about war and the pity of it, about bombs falling and people dying, and calls it 'The Streets of Hanoi'. Another man sets it to music. When the song is performed in public it appears on the programme as 'The Streets of Saigon'. No one has brought any pressure upon poet or composer; no one thinks the change of title anything but sensible. In any case, as we have noticed, the present climate is not conducive to martyrdom, however determined the candidate may be.

The silencing of writers under Communism in Russia might be considered altogether more momentous because

there are more writers to be silenced. But there is also a
tradition of writing there, it is in the blood: particular
writers get into trouble, but writing doesn't. Whereas in the
new countries the very idea of writing as a serious occupation
for a grown man is still in its frail and precarious childhood,
and the faintest intimidation on the part of the powers that
be can prove more efficaciously deterrent than the outright
savagery of the régime in older countries.

I don't want to make heavy weather of this question – it
has been touched on directly or indirectly elsewhere in this
book. I have no particular axe to grind, no vested interests
here, but just a nagging and sick little feeling that before you
ask people to fight for freedom, you should make sure they
have some. In conclusion, I would merely reiterate that our
literary and cultural panjandrums might occasionally lift
their ears from the listening posts along the Iron Curtain and
reflect for a moment on the odd and surely unnatural silence
in some other parts of the globe.

From time to time, coming across a poem of mine in an
English magazine, I would stop and wonder what on earth
it was doing there. No doubt others did too. It is of course
ludicrous to complain about the unfavourable reception of
one's work, or about not being understood, which more
often than not is one's own fault. But what has struck me
rather painfully is the consistent and blank lack of interest in
my subject-matter, the utter incuriosity on this score – for
me, the important one. One would have thought that however poetic fashions might change, there would always be a
small place for poetry of description and comment.

There were times (if I may be allowed this confession in
what, after all, are personal reminiscences) when I came to
think that I must be suffering from a curiously roundabout
or oblique paranoia, dreaming up wild tales of persecution,
not persecution of myself (obviously I wasn't doing too
badly) but of shadowy and mysterious others. And to
suspect, too, that my English readers, whoever they were,

must be humouring me gently. They might reproach me for deficiencies of style and poverty of technique, but they turned a kindly blind eye to this larger lapse. I began to fancy that I was off my head in a harmless sort of way, that Japanese saké, Thai opium and Singapore sun had finally undone me, and I was describing and commenting on things which simply *did not exist*.

What kept me soldiering on, usefully or not, were occasional letters from Africans, living in different African states, telling me how closely some poem or other described a situation they were experiencing in their own country, expressing surprise that I wasn't writing out of some African experience of my own, and surmising that despite what they had supposed, life in Asia ran parallel to life in Africa. It was this – together with a maturely muted irritation which I was still conscious of provoking in some quarters in Singapore – which gave me to hope that perhaps I wasn't entirely deranged, that perhaps nonetheless I was talking about realities, about the realities of some real people. Poetry or not, that didn't matter so much, but I hated to think that I was telling stories which were both tedious and tall.

To return to England, then? To that nest of stinging birds. To London and its affluent addiction to fashions of the flimsiest kind, with built-in obsolescence, created by the illiterate and legitimized by the bored, to with-itry and what-can-be-cleverly-talked-about (the brave new criterion in the free-from-politics world of the arts in Britain). An addiction, too, which is not redeemed by its heavy lining of self-protective cynicism: you can make a living out of peddling fashion and also out of the fashion of thoughtfully ridiculing fashion, practically simultaneously. Society believes in covering its bets.

It's probably too late to go back. One is too old to adjust to such spirited younkers as Malcolm Muggeridge. Already one finds whole tracts of such journals as the *New Statesman* and *The Spectator* largely incomprehensible. Perhaps, again, that is merely a reflection on oneself. Yet these are papers which were once, not so long ago, read with excitement in these far-flung regions. What they said had immediate significance here. Now they seem to be written largely in a private and indecipherable code, in a language without meaning, alien and irrelevant, to those who live outside the range of the British television services. The medium must indeed be the message, for precious little message gets through to us.

The Commonwealth looks to the old mother-lion and sees a frisky if faked poodle. Perhaps, after all, it's better to have a Communist, real or imagined, on your doorstep than a dope peddler. Does it have to be one or the other?

But those who cry 'Sick! Sick!' are often themselves a long way from health. And very possibly England isn't half as trivial as it seems from a distance. These writer chappies, they always present such a bad image of their countries! I remember those remarks of Wordsworth, so aptly quoted by Richard Hoggart in his book, *The Uses of Literacy*:

> 'Reflecting upon the magnitude of the general evil, I should be oppressed with no dishonourable melancholy, had I not a deep impression of certain inherent and indestructible qualities of the human mind . . .'

And yet, even as I type these words, it is Singapore I am thinking of rather than England.

.   .   .   .   .

> *But we have to work at a destiny.*
> *We stumble now and then. Our nerves are sensitive.*
> *We strive to find our history,*
> *Break racial stubbornness,*
> *Educate the mass and Educated –*
> *Evacuate the disagreeable . . .*
> *Set all neatly down into Economy.*
> *There is little choice –*
> *We must make a people . . .*
>
> EDWIN THUMBOO

To stay in Singapore, then? Assuming, of course, that one retains the choice. (I have received hints and nods from elsewhere, including – which gave me special pleasure – an exploratory cable from the Vice-Chancellor of the University of the West Indies at one point. Perhaps they don't expect Professors to overflow with literary criticism, only assistant lecturers.)

Singapore is a one-party state, and the party is almost a one-man party. Mr. Lee says he wants 'a good lively opposition', but perhaps after all the only good opposition is a dead one, and he was being wittily paradoxical.

Wise in their generation, the people construe him so. For he has also given them to understand that, since by the very nature of Singapore there can be no Rightist opposition, what opposition there was would have to be Left of the P.A.P. And what lies to the left of the P.A.P. is Communism.

As it is, the Barisan Sosialis festers away miserably among the Chinese-educated, listening to Peking Radio, scrawling slogans on bus shelters, and getting picked up from time to time; and Communists lurk underground, as they always have, under some name or other, and always will. If they didn't exist, we would have to invent them.

But no one has been shot or beaten up for reasons of State. Singapore is a good country. The Government gets its own way. To a large extent its way is a good one. The Headmaster is inclined to be rather strict and his tongue has a rough side to it. But the school knows that if they managed to get rid of him, another and probably much worse Headmaster would be appointed in his place.

No one is shot or beaten up. This is one of the most stable and peaceful countries in Asia. Another is Malaysia. Rather to their mutual surprise, perhaps.

While writing the first draft of this passage I was playing Michael Tippett's oratorio, *A Child of Our Time*. 'Burn down their houses. Beat in their heads. Break them in pieces on the wheel.' That doesn't happen in Singapore.

Mouths are closed, but minds are ajar. If there were more

opportunity for public dissent, there might well be less
dissent in private. If Mr. Lee has failed to win the love of the
intellectuals – himself a Cambridge double First with star, he
may not believe that there are any other intellectuals in
Singapore – at least he hasn't sent tanks into the campus.
(There wouldn't be room for them, not with all the private
cars that clog the place up.)

The Government knows the problems and is devotedly
pursuing the solutions. If the University's eyes are turned in
upon its navel, then never mind, the Government will
import Israeli advisers. (From being the New York or,
according to taste, the Paris of Malaysia, we have now
become the Israel of South-East Asia.) The Government's
ends are good: maximum prosperity in a context of maximum independence. And the means to the ends do not
include shooting anyone, or dropping bombs on Egyptian
villagers. The Government gets its own way. An occasional
veiled threat will do the job, for when grievances are small,
courage looks ludicrous. It is merely childish petulance to
cast a full rice-bowl to the ground.

The Minister for Defence (as he then was) has given his
definition of the sort of play which the dramatists of Singapore ought to be writing. If the recipe doesn't sound very
appetizing, it is at least the opposite of the recipe for fashionable success, brief fame or notoriety, on the contemporary
London stage. Which gives it a sort of relative charm. No
move has been made to punish playwrights who depart from
the Minister's recipe. So far no one has departed from it, to
my knowledge, no one has abided by it so far.

The members of the Government are utterly honest. God
help anyone of them who was caught putting fifty cents into
his pocket! They are not in any obvious sense of the word
self-seeking. They have the rectitude of primitive socialists,
along with some of the priggishness. In the course of a
speech to the British Labour Party rally at Scarborough on
October 1, 1967, Mr. Lee gave a good thumbnail description
of Singapore:

N

'I do not pretend that we are an idyllic socialist community in South-East Asia. We still have the highest number of million-aires per ten thousand of population in South Asia. But we are one of a few places in Asia where there are no beggars, where nobody, old or young, dies of neglect and starvation. True, they are modest achievements but none the less precious to us.'

Any opposition to the P.A.P. would indicate extreme in-gratitude on the part of the voters. Right or Left, the opposi-tion would be bound to be in the wrong!

The free exchange of ideas? The freedom of the press? People thinking for themselves? One recalls the story Matthew Arnold told of the advice given to Shelley's wife when she was looking for a school for her son, 'Send him somewhere where they will teach him to think for himself,' and how she replied, 'Teach him to think for himself? Oh, my God, teach him rather to think like other people!' We have received even more provocation than Mrs. Shelley had. These amenities are expensive. People get shot. And who really appreciates them, these luxury goods, but the spoilt liberal? Who but he, in his book-lined study, could suppose that, left to themselves, undisturbed by such agitators as he himself and his books, people would want freedom?

We shall settle for peace and prosperity, and death only in bed or on the roads. Happy the country that needs no heroes. Happy the times that are tidy – as Sylvia Plath said,

> ... the children are better for it,
> The cow milk's cream an inch thick.

24

Australia and China

DURING the university vacation in early 1963 I spent five weeks in Australia on a lecture tour sponsored by the British Council. The idea originated with the Council's Representative in Australia, a good friend of mine, and the home office, having in the meanwhile had further proof of my proneness to accident and scandal, was noticeably less enthusiastic about it. Acting on instructions from London, the British Council Representative in Singapore, another friend of mine but also a sensible man, came to me in some embarrassment to say that the Council in London would like some sort of assurance from me that while in Australia I would say nothing which might imperil or jeopardize their relations with Asian countries and more particularly with Mr. Lee Kuan Yew.

My friend and I agreed between ourselves that since, newspapers being what they were (and, according to some, Australian ones being even more so), no assurance could be given that whatever I did say would be correctly reported, there seemed no point in giving an assurance that I would not say anything that might prove offensive. I was a literary and academic visitor, and in fact political topics never arose in public during my tour. Except once, when a reporter for a local paper called on me at St. Mark's College in Adelaide. My friend the Representative in Sydney had given me a bottle of whisky to help me on my way and, understanding that Australians and newspaper men and hence Australian newspaper men especially were fond of drinking, I opened it. But while the alcohol had the effect of making me loquacious on South-East Asian politics and indeed quite brilliantly incisive (or so it seemed, and I only wish I could remember what I said), it brought about somnolence and amnesia in the reporter, for not a word of the long interview ever appeared in the press.

I found the great majority of Australians extremely kind and hospitable, which was just as well since at times some of them could be quite distinctly unkind – or rather, which betrays their Anglo-Saxon origins, frank and forthright. Like the man at a poetry reading who kept interrupting me with increasing wrathfulness to ask where the rhyme and metre had got to. Feelings run high in Australia against free verse and such-like literary liberties, and God help the poor devil who can't vindicate himself metrically! Then there was a lecture I gave at Sydney University on Edward Thomas, and the loud-voiced and large and bearded young man who in question time gave his opinion that Thomas was 'just another of those pommy bastard nature poets – tea on the vicarage lawn, and all that . . .' Afterwards, while the sherry was circulating, I asked him what year he was in. He wasn't a student, he exclaimed fiercely, he was writing a thesis for the master's degree, on James Joyce. Then he went on a shade more amicably to declare that it wasn't just pommy bastard nature poetry he was against, but all nature poetry. A little later, while I was listening with rather more interest to a girl student telling me that I looked like Harpo Marx and had a cleft chin which meant I couldn't help but run after women, I heard the voice of the young man raised over on the far side of the room. Someone had been chiding him for his tactless use of that common but hurtful expression, and he cried out, 'But I didn't know he was a pommy bastard himself!' He glared in my direction, his eyes red with rage at the imposture. 'I thought he was a Malay of some sort!'

But on the whole politeness easily won the day. There was no reproach even when by some accident I found myself giving the same lecture twice on the same day to substantially the same audience, an embarrassment aggravated by the fact that contrary to my calculations a book containing the lecture was already circulating in the country.

As for the myth of the tough, unreflecting and untroubled Aussie . . . The people I met, chiefly teachers and writers it must be admitted, struck me as rather more than normally neurotic and life-tormented, and the very reverse of tight-lipped. But then, people tend to talk more freely to a transient, a passer-through, they use him as a travelling dustbin for odd sorrows and little guilts. And moreover, I had grown accustomed to the reticent Chinese, who know that by talking about your troubles you make them harder to bear. Yet perhaps the myth was neither less nor more true than the legend about taxi-drivers which I had come across in a traveller's guide. This manual warned one sternly that in Australia a solitary male passenger should be sure to seat himself in the front beside the driver, since to sit alone in the back would be regarded as filthy rotten snobbishness, and also that one should not seek to tip the cabbie because Australians were proud folk and just as good as the next man if not better. The first time I took a taxi in Sydney I sought to insert myself matily in the front, but the driver gave me a queer look and said laconically, 'In the back, mate!' When paying up, I remarked that I was a stranger and had read in a book that it was not the custom to tip Australian taxi-drivers . . . He must have heard about this book before, since he didn't wait for the end of my sentence. 'I'm not Australian, mate,' he said, 'I am Hungarian!' On the second occasion I opened the front door of the cab only to find the seat piled high with books. This time the cabbie was a young German, working his way through college. What the book forgot to mention was that not many taxi-drivers in Australia are Australian.

Which reminds me that I met at Sydney University one of my old pupils from Japan, now teaching in the Department of Oriental Studies there. This is one of the special joys of mendicancy. If one is never entirely at home, nor is one ever entirely a stranger. There is bound to be someone whom one once taught or tried to teach. And happily, as Brecht's Herr Keuner implied, the pupils forget the master's failings long before he himself ceases to remember them.

In early 1965 I spent a short holiday in Hong Kong with David Rawlinson, a colleague of mine. Though Kowloon, where we were staying, showed some signs of life, albeit shabby ones, Hong Kong impressed us as a non-place. Or rather two non-places, one containing Chinese, the other containing Europeans, or non-Chinese. Coming from the Chinese city of Singapore, we found it rather gruesome to have no contact with the Hong Kong Chinese except on the strictly business basis of customer and waiter or client and tailor. An English acquaintance there, seeking to remind his wife of a particular party they had attended, one of many, said, 'You remember, darling – there were some Chinese there!' No doubt all concerned were quite satisfied with this state of affairs, for the Chinese were not likely to suppose themselves the inferiors of the Europeans, nor the other way about. But after three or four days of this non-living in a non-place, we decided we might as well do the tourist thing and go to Macao, until someone told us that we might just conceivably get visas in time for a short visit to Canton. We applied, and our visas arrived with surprising celerity. Feeling doubtful whether the Singapore authorities would approve of the trip, we went to some trouble to have the Chinese visas stamped on a detachable sheet of paper instead of on our passports – a service which the Chinese authorities are accustomed to offering intrepid American nationals. However, the stolid immigration officials at the British border post, Lo Wu, applied their stamp direct to the passport, and there was only one place you could possibly be going to from Lo Wu.

Arriving at Canton we were taken in charge by a peculiarly unintelligent official guide. Possibly it was nervousness (which we did nothing to foster) that caused him to seem more stupid than he was. He could be said to be devoted in that he didn't let us out of his sight during the two days we spent in Canton, except after he had delivered us into our grandiose Victorian bedrooms. There appeared to be no one else in this great barracks of a tourist hotel except a troupe of Pakistani cultural performers and out of deference to somebody or some ruling they were on a different floor. Although a bottle of the local brew was on display in the dining room, we at first found difficulty in procuring beer – a sense of viciousness obviously attached to it – but I felt reassured on our last day when, as we came in for a very early breakfast, a small boy rushed up smiling eagerly to ask whether we wouldn't like some beer. We wouldn't, but we had the satisfaction of feeling that even in so short a time we had done a little towards humanizing the atmosphere.

Most of our first day we spent looking round a big and varied exhibition of Goods for Export. The garments on display showed no tendency towards extremity of fashion, they were strongly reminiscent of the more conservative members of the British or the Japanese royal family. The sedate middle-length skirts and jumpers and the loaf-like hats in austere pinks and blues passed our guide's scrutiny, but the high-heeled shoes drew a gibe. 'Then why do you make them?' we naturally enquired. 'For export,' he said grimly, 'For export to other countries. We are too serious to wear such things here.' I asked him whether the cheongsam was in favour, and he reflected for a while and then said, 'Yes, cheongsam is permitted. Of course. It is traditional Chinese dress.' Traditions, as we know, are good things, but I remarked that we hadn't seen a single example of that charming garb in Canton. In truth we hadn't seen a woman dressed in anything other than blue or grey trousers. 'In Peking,' he answered shiftily, 'You see cheongsam in Peking, sometimes, in the evening.'

But on both evenings we were lucky enough to see excellent troupes of acrobats, much appreciated by audiences of working men and wives and children. The technical skill of the performers, that is to say, was first-class; the subject matter occasionally sank to a very low level of propaganda. One act showed a soldier trying to get in some target practice by aiming at a fellow soldier standing on a mound, but of course he couldn't bring himself to shoot. The other soldier then turned his cap around to show American army insignia and put on a pair of horn-rimmed Harold Lloyd-style spectacles, whereupon of course the first soldier found himself able to shoot, and after an acrobatic sequence in which he writhed comically, pulled funny faces and crossed himself grotesquely, the second soldier fell to the ground shot to pieces. The audience was very well-behaved, unlike the irreverent and talkative Chinese audiences we knew in Singapore, but they and the children enjoyed in their quieter way the making of the sign of the cross.

The children were very sweet. Small children, with protective gauze masks across nose and mouth, they would shoot an expressionless glance at us, quickly turning away as if we were some sort of unfortunate creatures or natural freaks which shouldn't be stared at. How foul that they should be subjected to this brutish propaganda! I tried to think of the brainwashing I'd undergone at their age. Nothing half as carbolic as this, no – just that it was merely right and proper to die for your king and country, that when there wasn't a war there was unemployment which was less stirring and worse for the country, that on Empire Day you saluted the flag and sang a special hymn, that foreigners were silly and wicked, that too much reading was bad for the eyes and other parts of you as well, and that God intended you to abide in that state of life to which He had called you, with the exception of a few scholarship boys who would have to be eternally grateful to society for going against God on their behalf... Oh well, perhaps those sweet little things would grow up to love Americans, Christians, sex and high-heeled shoes – and to hate acrobats.

The high standard of behaviour among the audience – except on the part of our guide who was sitting in front and turned round to grin at us whenever the agit-prop came on:

he certainly wasn't one of those who repair to church for the
music there – was positively intimidating. We were even
relieved to find one old railway worker hawking and
spitting away – just as, passing a roller-skating rink on our
way to the theatre, I had felt relieved (indeed my dried-up
little bourgeois heart dropped a warm tear) to see a man and
a woman gliding round the rink hand in hand. Except that
when they came round the next time I was forced to perceive
that they were both women.

Our conscientious guide proposed to take us to inspect
either a collective farm or a steel works. We explained that
we wouldn't be able to tell a good farm or steel works from
a bad one, and that what we would really like to visit, if it
were possible, would be a school, secondary or primary, or
better still a university. That would be very difficult to
arrange, he told us, but he would make a few phone calls
nonetheless. He came back to ask our exact ranks and
functions at the University of Singapore, and finally re-
appeared to tell us, incredulously, that it had been agreed
that we should visit Sun Yat Sen University that very
afternoon.

This was the most interesting part of our Cantonese
experience. Especially after it was discovered that, among
many ancient anthologies of great thoughts and literary
beauties, the library contained a textbook I had co-edited.
The Dean of Foreign Languages, a Cambridge graduate,
was a canny functionary, but the younger teachers were
pleasant, friendly, interested, and one felt that under slightly
different circumstances and with more time we might have
approached something like frankness. The atmosphere
reminded me vividly of the many earnest discussions I had
attended in Japan, at a long table, over tea and cigarettes,
with the interrogators speaking in order of seniority. Their
problem here was to teach English language, and they were
not especially interested in literature, except as an aid to
language. They wanted to know how we did it in Singapore,
and clearly they didn't believe us when we said that we

didn't teach language there since the great majority of our students had been educated from the start in the medium of English. 'But they *are* Chinese,' they reiterated reproachfully, as if it were axiomatic that no Chinese would speak English without having been subjected to some very special technical process. It looked as if we were selfishly concealing a secret recipe for the instilment of English into Chinese students, so I confessed that we did run a course in English language for a few students admitted from Chinese-medium schools, but we had no particular technique, we just read things to them and got them to write things. 'Ah, British empiricism!' one of them exclaimed, and general satisfaction was felt at this neat and face-saving encapsulation.

The Dean was not so pleased when I incautiously alluded to the bad habit of some of our students of hiding books on the wrong shelves in the library so that they could find them at will but no one else could. 'Wrong motivation!' he said scornfully. And as we were walking in the grounds of the University and he pointed to a large empty space where once a law faculty had stood, I mentioned that in Singapore we had a large Faculty of Law. 'You would, yes, you would!' he said with an oddly personal vehemence. 'Property law, divorce law – but we don't have either of those here, so we don't need any law!' In the library, David Rawlinson had been describing our first-year syllabus and he asked a young lecturer whether they taught D. H. Lawrence in Canton. 'No,' gasped the young Chinese, reeling backwards into the book-stacks of Dickens, Shaw and Galsworthy, 'Oh no, no! Our students are very young when they come up, they are only twenty-five!'

We were asked to tape-record something for use in teaching; J. B. Priestley had passed through a little earlier and recorded the first chapter of *The Good Companions*, they told us. A copy of the *Oxford Book of English Verse* was produced and I asked them to choose something for me to read. After some polite to-and-fro, the Dean asked for Julian Bell, and a certain loss of face was incurred all round when it proved that there was nothing by Julian Bell in the *Oxford Book*. So I read Marvell's poem, 'To his Coy Mistress', content in the knowledge that I couldn't possibly be lending myself to any ideological misuse of English literature. The students would probably be considered too young to listen to it.

Our guide might now have acquired a new respect for us as people before whom university doors were at once thrown open, but he seemed more nervous than ever. He had frequently accepted a cigarette from me and so, since he was clearly less amenable to tipping than Australian cabbies, I offered him a full packet of some English cigarettes as we were saying goodbye at the railway station. He pushed it aside fearfully: 'No, no, I do not smoke!'

If Canton was a change from Hong Kong, then Hong Kong, we felt when we got back to it, was a change from Canton. And, for all its stresses and strains, Singapore was the best change of all. How good it was, we reflected, to be back among the Chinese!

A few days after returning to Singapore I received an invitation to become a sponsor of the recently formed Society for Anglo-Chinese Understanding. With these Cantonese experiences and non-experiences in mind, as well as an old interest in and respect for the Chinese, I felt glad to accept. Understanding seemed to me an admirable and much-needed thing all round. I let my membership lapse in the following year when it became fairly plain that the 'understanding' in question was strictly one-way and to be erected on a foundation of misinformation or misinterpretation amounting to deceit. I had supposed that a realization of the truth or of a decent part of it would be the sufficient aim of the Society, since China's past wrongs and present difficulties were of such an order as to account largely for her internal disorders and external hostilities. As Dennis Bloodworth has put it, to have known the face is to understand the face-lift.

But before long the Society's leading spirits were representing these disorders and hostilities as positively and unexceptionably desirable. Such an attitude in educated people could only be hypocritical. Understanding had yielded to a factitious acclamation. The Chinese seem to me far too lively, too intelligent, too important and certainly too formidable to be patronized in this childish way.

25

Apology for Mendicancy

IN December 1966 I went a second time to Hong Kong, to attend a conference on English as a University Subject in the Western Pacific Area. This was the first conference I had ever taken part in; though South-East Asia throbs with academic get-togethers, my subject is underprivileged conferentially. Or perhaps privileged by being thus underprivileged. The cumulative effect of this particular conference, I should say, was to confirm everyone just a little more obstinately or bitterly in the views he originally held. At least that was the effect on me; it was disconcerting to emerge from the ivory tower and find the most extreme of one's paranoiac imaginings taking real and human shape. The conference in Hong Kong had no sooner assembled than it split into a number of barely reconcilable groups, ranging from those who were totally preoccupied with the problems of teaching huge classes of Thai science students a little basic English to those interested in the techniques of Practical Criticism, from the pros and cons of creative translation or literary 'imitations' to the difficulty of getting 'th' sounded properly. And underneath or over all extended the ominous cleft between teachers of literature (sometimes hideously referred to as 'littérateurs') and experts in linguistics, and that mutual hostility which only the linguisticians, insolently charitable in the knowledge of approaching victory, deny the existence of.

The teacher of literature is inevitably something of a missionary. (What is wrong with that? We grew up believing it was only right and proper to have a mission in life. Yes, but it was a long time ago that we were growing up.) The language teacher on the other hand is a technician, he is concerned with words, but not with their meaning. The literature teacher actually wants his pupils to be changed by literature; the language teacher merely wants them to be made more efficient members of a given society, to fit in more neatly, to be more efficient citizens. It will readily be understood that what the leaders of the new countries want is efficiency, and that what they don't want is to have the native hue of resolution sicklied o'er with the pale cast of English literature. For literature deals in ideas and feelings, precepts and examples, which are not inevitably conducive to the smooth running of the State. Not here! Not now! When a Prime Minister jeers at foreign poetry about daffodils, he doesn't really believe that literature is meant to be a repository of botanical information, he isn't being silly, he has his reasons. Living for politics himself, proliferating politics all around him, he expects literature to be read politically.

The growing ascendancy of language teaching (the provision of means) over literature teaching (the examination of ends) is only another instance of what seems to be happening all over the world. We have lost faith in ourselves, without acquiring humility; the measure of our self-contempt is that before long we may be finally content to be 'realistic'. Recognizing no ends further than survival, we must make means the whole of our faith. Blessed are the simple-minded, for they shall inherit the earth. But not the libraries: they must be burnt, except for technical books. Then we can safely embrace the second childhood of our species, reasonably well fed and cared for, rocking gently between one simple duty and another. As a liberal and a teacher of literature, I sometimes suspect that, rather unfairly, I am a member of two dying races!

I have so often been called upon to defend my profession that of late I have fallen back on flippancy. Whatever the circumstances may be, the person who requires you to justify the greatest body of literature the world has known is not going to be won over by solemn reasoning. I propose to conclude this book with the short paper I contributed to the conference in Hong Kong. In manner it is somewhat light-hearted – an air not unfitting to men who have their backs to the wall – but possibly it possesses a little of that 'underlying seriousness' which an occasional kindly reviewer has allowed me in the past. If he wishes, the reader may regard my remarks on The Teaching of English Literature Overseas as in the nature of an appendix which only the rare surviving specialist would wish to consult. In that case he should pass to the second appendix, immediately preceding the back cover. Personally, though, I feel that the paper finds a proper place here as a memoir, a distillation however volatile of experience, and also an apology of sorts for my mendicant life.

In any case a brisk and business-like finish is to be desired. No reader, however zealous his scientific curiosity, can persevere very long with the animadversions of a disillusioned liberal. Disillusioned – and yet with no superior illusion in view, and so perhaps not to be accurately called 'disillusioned'. 'Chastened' let us rather say. What you have not deified cannot fail you so utterly. As for 'liberal', I don't think it will ever come to seem a dirty word to me.

The Daffodil Transplanted

I want to begin by quoting two speakers at the Conference on the Teaching of English Literature Overseas which was held in Cambridge under the auspices of the British Council in July 1962. Firstly, two remarks made by a British professor from a British university. 'Literature is useful even in language learning'; and, 'If they can't cope with the best, let them cope with the second-best.' Secondly, some remarks made by an Indian professor from an Indian institution. 'We go to English literature because it is a great literature . . . English literature has a variety of modern world classics – works which concentrate on the fundamental problems of human life in a modern or contemporary manner . . . In this sense English literature ceases to be English. It is simply literature . . .'

The first speaker's remark – 'If they can't cope with the best, let them cope with the second-best' – with its regrettable reminiscence of Marie Antoinette, its patronizingly breezy tone, would seem to indicate an alarming insensitiveness to the English language – for I am sure that the speaker didn't mean to be offensive to the very persons, the overseas students of English literature, who were the *raison d'être* of the Conference. Malcolm Muggeridge is not the only person, indeed not the first, to surmise that the last surviving English gentlemen are Indians. It even looks as if India will be the last place where English literature is to survive! Despite which, we go on debating whether English literature is a fit or feasible subject for teaching in India – I am now using India symbolically – and whether India is a fit or feasible place for English literature to be taught in. An analysis of the emotions and attitudes involved in this debate, by the way, would produce some scandalous findings on both sides of the house: contempt for foreigners, contempt for literature, a cynical belittlement of the imagination, vested interests, laziness, megalomania, ignorance and incompetence, inability to learn from experience, sycophancy, over-readiness to bow before political breezes . . . One decent attitude would be honest doubt. Is there any one of us who has never felt any doubt, if not about ends then at least about means? *Ends.* 'Gad, she'd better!' was Carlyle's comment on the lady who decided to accept the universe. He only had to make that comment once; and now it features in most dictionaries of quotations. If he had had to repeat it, as often as those of us who see nothing inevitably criminal or ludicrous in the teaching of English literature overseas have had to defend our views, then he might have found it difficult to maintain that first crisp cogency! However, here goes . . .

Professor V. K. Gokak, the Indian professor whom I quoted, has gone to the heart of the matter. English literature is a great literature, certainly the greatest of the English arts, possibly the greatest of all literatures. It has depth and it has breadth – a breadth, a variety, which we have come to take for granted. Compare it, for instance, with German literature, which is famous for its depth of course but seems to me to possess comparatively little variety, or with Japanese literature, which has a long history (what is probably the best Japanese novel was written around A.D. 1,000) but still, I would venture, not very much diversity whether of philosophy, attitude, tone or technique. Also, as Professor Gokak points out, English literature is a modern literature, it has (despite its periods of local stagnation) moved with the times and been a part of the thought of its time; it has not (like some Eastern literatures) been regarded as a special, unworldly and sacrosanct activity which is the more highly esteemed the more remote it is from the everyday, the merely temporal, the merely human; it has not been tied to any religion or to any social class for long, and except for a few inconsiderable practitioners there has been nothing of the element of 'cult' about it. In short, it is a notably open and accessible literature, and on the whole a free literature, too

rich in 'traditions' for any single tradition to manage to erect
itself into a law and a tyranny. I don't mean to imply that the
English writer has had a soft time of it, has been luckier than
he deserves – the creation of literature isn't easy, any more
than the teaching of it – but I would suggest that the English
reader is luckier than he, than we, commonly acknowledge.
Familiarity – and this is the teacher's danger – can come to
breed a most inapt contempt.

English literature, then, offers a vast reservoir of human
experience and of judgment of experience, a development of
imagination, an entry into human situations which otherwise might well fall outside our ken . . . But there is no need
for this high-falutin' rhetoric from me, when two little
stories will tell the tale. The first concerns a most remarkable
piece of equipment, a new aid to rapid learning, which I read
about several years ago. This apparatus has no electric
circuit to go wrong, it is easy to handle (even a child can
use it) and is readily portable. It is known as BUILT-IN
ORDERLY ORGANIZED KNOWLEDGE, and in the
modern fashion its makers call it by its initials – B–O–O–K
. . . That story, I confess, I have stolen from *Punch*, but the
second is more truly my own, since it has to do with a
student at Chulalongkorn University in Bangkok and the
essay which she wrote for me on the theme, The Place of
Literature in the Modern World. Her opening sentence went
as follows: 'The place of literature in the modern world, I am
sure, is England, since that is where English literature,
especially Shakespeare, is written.'

Granted all that, the objection may be raised that we are
supposed to be talking about the *teaching* of literature, and
more specifically the teaching of English literature in the
Western Pacific Area (or what to my unscientific or romantic
mind is the Far East). I intend to evade the first of the
questions which this objection poses, the question of the
possibility or otherwise of teaching literature at all, by
suggesting that in these days no body of knowledge or
speculation (however orderly, however organized) will be

taken seriously unless it features as a university subject, and that, if you take a look at some of the subjects which are creeping or rather storming into university calendars, you are likely to tell yourself, Gad, we'd better accept literature as a teaching subject! Put it this way: maybe you can't make a horse drink, but at least you can take him to the water.

As for the teaching of English literature in the East or the Far East or in Africa, basically there is little more to say than I have already said. As a great literature, it can legitimately be taught in countries which have their own literature. Where the indigenous literature is not 'modern', where material life has become modern but social and spiritual life hasn't yet caught up with it, there will be all the more need for English literature (with what Professor Gokak calls its 'modernizing influence') to be taught. Our exports shouldn't be lop-sided. We all know the sort of Briton, met at cocktail parties, who finds something irresistibly funny in the fact that one is hired to teach English literature in Singapore, say. Such people, as I suggested in a magazine symposium several years ago, 'are usually the same people who see nothing either comic or disturbing about our export eastwards of Worcester sauce, china shepherdesses, vibro-massage, TV, horror films and armaments.' In comparison I was quite captivated by the gentleman who, on learning my profession, told me altogether seriously that I must be sorely troubled in my conscience since I was imparting knowledge to the Chinese, a race who were already overknowledgeable. I assured him that English literature was a notoriously debilitating influence.

Thirdly comes the kind of country which has little or no indigenous literature as yet, which must in any case take its reading matter from abroad for the time being. In Singapore and Malaysia there are many who are unable to read Chinese literature, or unable to obtain full satisfaction from it, and as for Malay literature, there doesn't seem to be much of it to read. For a growing majority of people, if they are to study literature at all, it will have to be literature in English, and for some time to come predominantly English literature. I hope that no one is going to say, 'If they don't have a literature of their own, then let them study economics . . .' Perhaps this is the point at which to remark that, though it is not the primary object of teaching English literature to produce or foster local writers in these new countries, such will be a secondary effect of the study of the subject. As I have already implied, English literature seems as good a foster-parent in this respect as there is, simply because of its diversity, its freedom from absolutes, and the stress it lays on individuality and experimentation, on social relevance and the changing needs of changing times. All models can be abused, of course: English literature at least offers so many different models as to discourage the potential abuser as far as he can be discouraged.

Now for the objections. The commonest has to do with the student's lack of 'inwardness' with the language. Obviously there is an element of truth here: the more a language means to you in your everyday life, the more it will mean when it takes the form of literature. At the same time we shouldn't make a shibboleth of this 'inwardness': to explain connotations of words (and at times denotations!) is what the teacher is there for – and I find that students generally catch on quite quickly. If we can't provide every student with the 'bed-dictionary' which (I gather) was much in favour with diplomats of an earlier day, then we can offer him something almost as good, perhaps even better in some ways – literature, the beloved of language. A native English-man would be hard put to it to say how much his inwardness with his own language comes from using it continuously from an early age and how much derives from reading the literature of the language. Literature and life go together, the one inseparably interwoven with the other; and as the British professor was kind enough to allow, 'literature is useful even in language learning.'

The second common objection has to do with the student's

lack of background knowledge. Hence my title: we all know the sad story, ascribed to various nationalities, of the overseas student, a specialist in Wordsworth, who came to England and apostrophized a bank of dandelions under the impression that they were daffodils . . . Had the student been a botanist there might be reason for the mirth and horror which this anecdote has provoked – a reaction, incidentally, not unlike that which in earlier times was provoked by Shakespeare's attribution to Bohemia of a sea coast.

> *Others in Elysian valleys dwell,*
> *Resting weary limbs at last on beds of asphodel*

– the lines haven't lost their charm since Robert Graves informed us that in fact the asphodel is 'a hardy, tall, tough, unscented and commercially valueless plant,' and therefore more remote from our poetic conception of the asphodel than is the dandelion from the daffodil. Talking of background knowledge, how many British readers have seen a lotus, or could recognize a phoenix? How many (whether virginal or not) have encountered a unicorn? These forms of life exist in poetry and by virtue of the poetry, and the same is true of the particular daffodils in Wordworth's poem. They are golden, they are beside the lake, beneath the trees, and they are fluttering and dancing in the breeze. It was Rilke who described the unicorn as 'the creature which is not', and went on to say,

> *Not there, because they loved it, it behaved*
> *as though it were. They always left some space.*
> *And in that clear unpeopled space they saved*
> *it lightly reared its head . . .*
> > *They fed it, not with corn,*
> *but only with the possibility*
> *of being. And that was able to confer*
> *such strength, its brow put forth a horn. One horn . . .*

Naturally a certain amount of explanation will always be necessary. That is what teachers are for, to help with the understanding of the work. This may mean conveying historical information. Professor Gokak was right again when he remarked that 'one can enjoy a masterpiece like *Macbeth* without knowing anything about medieval Scotland.' But even an occasional British reader will have to find out or be told the precise nature of the reference to the seven sleepers' den in Donne's 'The Good Morrow'. The reaction of Singapore students generally goes along these lines: 'I don't know exactly what the seven sleepers' den is – it must be some story, perhaps in the Bible – but I get the general idea, that the lovers feel they must have been asleep until they fell in love . . .' Which, I dare say, is a widespread sort of reading response: near enough is good enough. One student, when I pressed him for something more precise, ventured that the seven sleepers' den was an opium den – which is not a bad guess, after all: it suits quite well with the overall meaning of the poem. We recognize that the teacher will have to do a good deal of work which he wouldn't need to at a corresponding level in the home country – including vocabulary work. Students have come to distrust dictionaries, especially where words in poetry are concerned! But the objection to the teaching of English literature in the East because of its 'foreignness' seems to assume firstly that the students lack imaginative capacity and secondly that they lack teachers of English literature, or else their teachers are totally failing in the most obvious aspects of their duty! *Some*, of course, do; *some*, of course, are.

Since earlier on I used the word *ends*, I must at least let drop the other word, *means*. I have implied that the chief means in the teaching of literature is the teacher. Just as there is no substitute for literature, so there is no substitute for the teacher of it. Amateur dramatics are perhaps more valuable to the actors than to the audience. The drawback as regards films or professional stage productions is that they may 'fix' one's imaginative conception of the play – so that, for instance, Hamlet is forever after Sir Laurence Olivier, or Antony is Marlon Brando – especially at an early stage in one's reading. But possibly I am now myself falling into the error of supposing overseas students to be more fragile, more vulnerable, than they often are. When the New Shakespeare Company played in Singapore in 1965 local opinion was unanimous in finding the production of *The Taming of the Shrew* acceptable and that of *The Tempest* downright poor. My own complaint about the use of recordings of poetry and plays is that the gramophone or tape-recorder so often goes wrong – unlike the B-O-O-K – and the class's time is wasted. Otherwise recordings can be distinctly valuable – as can also the teacher's reading aloud of poetry and his encouragement of the students to do likewise. More than the native reader, foreign readers of a literature tend to read with the eye alone, as their eccentric scansion sometimes indicates. Local differences in accentuation have to be watched for. For example, the word 'academic' is often to be heard in Singapore as 'acádemic', which lends it a little extra seediness, especially in such contexts as 'acádemic freedom'. No, the teacher shouldn't be ashamed to read poetry to his students – it is one quite potent means to the elucidation of the poetry's meaning.

The choice of texts to be studied will of course vary with the language capacities as well as the mental capacities of one's students. Though considered the most subtle of word-users, Shakespeare is also the most amenable to reading at almost every level of language-knowledge. Then, if the staff-student ratio permits, the stress should be on tutorials rather than lectures; with some work done at any rate at later stages of development in Practical Criticism, this exercise to be carried out, as ever, with discretion.

I haven't dwelt on the difficulties we face, the disappointments we suffer, because we all know about them. They are ponderables – but we also know that they exist in a context of imponderables. We recognize our failures, but we cannot estimate at all accurately our successes. Finally, as I've suggested, we teach literature because there is as yet no substitute for it. T. S. Eliot described literary criticism as 'an instinctive activity of the civilized mind' – how much more so, how much less ambiguously so, are writing and reading! The miseries of teaching literature, whether at home or abroad, are inextricably intertwined with the splendours. W. H. Auden's lines about the writing of poetry, in his memorial poem for Louis MacNeice, seem in their stoicism and wry pride to have some applicability also to the teaching of poetry, of literature, in modern societies:

> *After all, it's rather a privilege*
> *amid the affluent traffic*
> *to serve this unpopular art which cannot be turned into*
> *background noise for study*
> *or hung as a status trophy by rising executives,*
> *cannot be 'done' like Venice*
> *or abridged like Tolstoy, but stubbornly still insists upon*
> *being read or ignored . . .*

Appendix 2

'The Truth is Concrete': Two Anecdotes

1. A young Greek woman to whom I gave English lessons in Alexandria in 1948 told me how she had come out from Greece a few years before to marry a well-to-do Alexandrian Greek merchant, a widower. One afternoon soon after her arrival she was sitting in a café on the Corniche with her young step-son. At a nearby table sat a noisy group of Egyptians in army uniform, one of whom, a fat man, ogled her strenuously. She ignored these attentions. The manager of the café came to her to say that one of the officers would like to make her acquaintance. She declined the invitation. He returned a little later to inform her that in fact the officer was the King, His Majesty King Farouk, and she would be well advised to accede to his request. 'The King is a pleasant gentleman,' pleaded the embarrassed manager. She shook her head. 'The King takes what he wants,' added the manager in a spirit of kindliness. She shook her head, and sat on over her coffee. 'Let's go home, mammy,' said the little boy. But she didn't see why she should be forced to leave before she was ready. She had only recently come from Greece. At last the little boy dropped the spoon with which he was eating his ice-cream and burst into tears, and so she had to take him home. He was an Alexandrian.

2. The home of an ordinary, peaceable man was entered one day by a large and violent person, a person of great power and authority, who asked the man: 'Do you agree to serve me?' Without saying a word the man prepared food and drink for this person, and gave him the best room in the house and the best bed to sleep on. Washing and mending his clothes, cooking his meals, cleaning up after him, the man of the house served the intruder assiduously and without a

218

word of complaint for seven years. At the end of this time the person of great power and authority had grown so fat, as fat even as the famous King of Egypt, and so unhealthy from lack of exercise that he died. The man wrapped the body in old sacking and threw it on a rubbish tip. Then he returned home, and burnt the bedding, washed the bedstead down with disinfectant, whitewashed the walls, scrubbed the floor-boards, and answered: 'No.' *(after Brecht)*